MW00966386

Gifts of Sisterhood

a journey on to your own

By

Patricia L. Brooks

www.giftsofsisterhood.com

St. Ignace to Scottsdale

authorHOUSE™

1663 LIBERTY DRIVE, SUITE 200
BLOOMINGTON, INDIANA 47403
(800) 839-8640
WWW.AUTHORHOUSE.COM

First published by AuthorHouse 02/21/05

ISBN: 1-4208-1875-9 (sc)

Library of Congress Control Number: 2004099884

Printed in the United States of America
Bloomington, Indiana

This book is printed on acid-free paper.

Back cover photo Szabo Photography
Family portrait on front cover by Cliff Ammons Photography

ACKNOWLEDGEMENTS

So many wonderful people contributed in various ways to the birthing of this book – some directly and some by just being in my life as a friend. I hereby acknowledge all of you for your support and trust that I would do my best.

I especially want to acknowledge my editor for her valuable assistance during the writing of this book. I could not have completed this work without her editorial expertise. My appreciation goes far beyond our business relationship. Her friendship and support during many days when I needed encouragement will always be remembered. She made my words come alive by letting me know I had something valuable to say about my sister's spirit.

I am eternally grateful to my family…especially to my parents for raising us in the Upper Peninsula of Michigan and giving me such a wonderful backdrop for this book. The memories and the stories that surround those days and our lives there will always be cherished parts of my life.

Thank you to my companion who stood by me night after night as I hid out in my home office writing and editing, and planning and praying over this piece of work. Thank you to him as well for critiquing this book with love and kindness.

Thank you to those who have supported me in my various writers' groups. Your guidance and ideas on this journey have helped me in more ways than I even know.

I greatly acknowledge my youngest sister for whom this book is dedicated. Without her, none of this insightfulness would have happened in this way. Thank you, as well, to my two other sisters who continue to be an important part of my life.

DEDICATION

I wish to dedicate this book to my sister for her wit, courage, charm and inspiration while she faced her greatest life challenge. Thank you, youngest sister, for letting me be me; for always being patient and positive; and for trusting in God to inspire us all. I believe this work is yours as well as mine, and I thank you again for your gifts of sisterhood. You truly have been my beacon of light on this journey of life.

Say only what is good and helpful to those you are talking to,

and what will give them a blessing.

The Book of Ephesians

PREFACE

Books are written for a lot of reasons: entertainment, distraction, teaching, information, self-discovery, history. This book is written to say thank you, I love you and God bless to my sister for her wit, courage, charm and inspiration, plus all the other gifts she gave so freely. Gifts I had to almost lose before I realized they were there for the taking and had always been there. Gifts I will treasure always and gifts I will share with you forever.

Smile and the world will belong to you. She had an infectious smile, one that more than lit up the room; one that was just mischievous enough that you were being warned that some quip or joke was about to materialize. She had a big toothy smile that perfectly matched the rest of her demeanor and attire - the laid-back approach to life. She knew a smile was an inexpensive way to enhance your looks and she used it often. That smile, that mischievous smirk, is seen in family portraits. One such picture was taken when I was about twelve and she was seven, and we four daughters posed for the first of many "sister" photos. It was the same smile seen again years later as we lined up on the long weathered fence rail near the Beach for yet another photo, and finally that special Christmas at the "big house" for what was to be our last family reunion photo to include more than just her spirit.

Blessed is he, who has learned to laugh at himself,
for he shall never cease to be entertained.

John Boswell

A great sense of humor is your best asset. Her sense of humor made her able to function for hours with jokes she had heard, funny jokes that fed off each other. Once she had us laughing, we knew it was not going to end anytime soon. She had more than a little of the Irish in her. Catholic jokes were her favorites!

As we have opportunity, let us do well to all people.

The Book of Galatians

A twinkle in your eye and spring in your step makes people want to follow you. Her eyes were like Mom's - wide, deep-set and hazel green/blue in color. They had that twinkle of a whimsical person. She never seemed rushed, but was always moving; some of that was her energy and some of that a nervousness all her own. Her wheels were always turning and running, making plans for her next move.

One of the best things someone can have up their sleeve is a funny bone.

Richard L. Weaver, II

Great wit is always appreciated. Her memory for all of us includes entertaining stories, ones of her and the family and her friends, and those stories of people she knew and liked. They were never vindictive stories or stories of planned revenge. She found humor in things that some of us miss. She appreciated the humanness in all of us, especially in herself.

It is of immense importance to learn to laugh at ourselves.

Katherine Mansfield

Be kind to animals and children and the world will see you as a humane person. Her love of animals was seen in her dogs, all five Cocker Spaniels that came in and out of her life during her 16 married years. Heidi and Annie came first, then Dylan, Patty McGee and Bailey's Irish Cream, the dogs "we loved to hate" only because of the preferential treatment they received from her. We used to laugh that the dogs were valued more by her than any of us, including her children. Her dogs were rarely if ever disciplined, but they were fed "people food" and allowed in places young children should be forbidden from most of the time. They were devoted to her. She liked to remind us that any time you think you have power and influence, try ordering around someone else's dogs! She was right, they never behaved for anyone else, but they loved and adored her, and missed her long after she was gone.

Appreciate your life just the way it is and life will be an adventure. She never took her life for granted. She lived life to the fullest. I remember on more than one occasion before Cancer came into our family her telling me how much she appreciated her life. That her life was so good she could have hardly imagined it would turn out this way. She loved living at "home" again in the North Country, in small town Americana – the Upper Peninsula of Michigan - near her friends and for a while our parents. She had turned her life around and life had improved because that is what happens to us when we let life take its course and take the action steps forward on that path, even if they are baby steps. She knew the trouble with being an optimist is that people think you do not know what is going on, but she did not care and kept going through many trying times with the attitude it takes to survive. She was able to laugh at herself and pick up the pieces over and over again, just as she did after her divorce, after dropping out of school, and after many dead-end jobs.

She never gave up, she never quit and she never asked for pity or for you to feel sorry for her anytime in her life. She knew there were people worse off than she was and that many would give anything to change places with her. She taught me to take a step back and to say thank you often. She allowed me to be me, and to relish in the fact that uniqueness is our greatest gift from God. And, so, this book is to you "little sister" for freeing me from my own self to be true to myself.

"Death is nothing at all – I have only slipped away into the next room. Whatever we were to each other, we are still today. Call me by my old familiar name; speak to me in the easy way which you always used. Laugh as we always laughed together. Play, smile, think of me, and pray for me. Let my name be the household name it always was to you. Let it be spoken. Life means all that it ever meant."

(Henry Scott Holland: 1847-1918 – found in a monastery in Ireland)

TABLE OF CONTENTS

CHAPTER ONE
The Gift of Compassion

To ease another's heartache is to forget one's own.

Abraham Lincoln

My sister was five years younger than me, the youngest of four daughters. She was the first one in the family to be born at the "new" local hospital. She was born at a time, the mid-1950's, when young children did not have visitation rights in a hospital so Dad took the rest us to the hospital window and held us above the deep and fluffy snow banks that crisp and cold morning - one typical of many January mornings in the Upper Peninsula of Michigan where the air is crystal clear and the bite of the temperature awakens the senses. Mom had tubes in her arms, chest and legs, as if ready for electric shock; they were never explained. Now the mother of four, she had her work cut out for her. My sister was born with a protruding "belly button" that we were told needed to be fixed.

- *She was the first one of the sisters to have surgery, and we began to understand compassion.* She was the one that had the most hospitalization and the most number of Doctors. Who could have known what God had in store and what lessons we were to learn about life? I still remember the day we picked her up after that "belly button" surgery, from a larger hospital about 50 miles away from home. It was about a year after she was born. She had a large bandage on her tummy where they had repaired the "belly button." She also had a sore on her lip from sucking her thumb for so long while at the hospital.

1

She must have felt somewhat alone during her stay in the hospital; but I don't remember her crying, just looking longingly at us as we looked up at her in Dad's arms. She had that same impish look that we saw so many times in family pictures. It was my first experience with compassion while feeling sorry it was her surgery and grateful it wasn't mine. She had her first of many scars and would be forever different from the rest of us.

- ***She was the first one to survive a serious accident, and we learned more about compassion.*** I still remember the time Mom called and said my sister was hit by a car while riding her bicycle home from high school on old Portage Road. She had quite a gash in her leg just behind the knee and forever a spider-like six inch scar; and then she was hit again the next year. It was the same time of year and a very similar accident. She saw this as a sign to be more careful, or was it a sign that our work in compassion was only beginning? I don't remember her complaining this time either. I don't remember who did this to her and why it happened twice; I just know it was not her time to leave us but an opportunity to feel compassion for someone experiencing pain, and shock of what could have been.

- ***She was the one left behind for her high school years.*** Her three older sisters, including myself, are between five and ten years older. By the time her high school years came along, we had been gone from the old homestead for some time. We all married quite young by today's standards. She had the run of the house for all those years of junior high and high school, and also the run of our parents. Sometimes the rest of us were envious or jealous but no one said a thing. It would have done no good. It surely made no difference in relationship to God's plan for all of us.

She didn't have to share a bedroom and bathroom with anyone else, or wear hand-me-down clothes. She didn't have to share the car with any of us. She had it made, or so we thought. It was the luck of the draw; and why not her? It had to be one of us. We had paved the way and she knew it. These years were her years of friends and parties, tears and fights - teenage years that are played out in most households. Mom and Dad may have been tired of raising four daughters or had finally developed some compassion for what it was like growing up in the 60's, because they fought her less and enjoyed her high school years more. She may have wanted more of a fight. Either way, she played her role and enjoyed her time there.

• *She was the one that came home and stayed to make her life in our small hometown.* She knew that growing up in small town America, in the Northern part of Michigan, the Upper Peninsula, the Straits of Mackinac was God's country and she could make a life there and a home and a difference. Her short experience of living in Denver is, in part, what again took her home and to a life with someone much like her. She made "home" available to all of us, that chance again to appreciate what we had growing up. Even if Ozzie and Harriet weren't at the helm. Dad had passed on from a third heart attack shortly after her second boy was born, he said he wasn't going anywhere until he saw his new grandchild and he wasn't kidding. Mom was suffering in her own world due to Alzheimer's disease at the same time.

3

My sister's world was busy with her boys and their friends, but she took time to help our parents in more ways than we will know yet still made home a welcomed spot to rest for vacation and to go back in time it was knowing that a step back in time was available that we will always cherish.

Cleaning your house while your kids are still growing is like clearing the drive before it has stopped snowing.

Phyllis Dillar

- *She was the one who had a home where we could always visit.* Her last home was to be back on the Straits of Mackinac just down the hill from the place where we grew up, in the familiarity of a childhood long gone. The place, Graham's Point, where we grew up and became "little women"was small in size with barely the basics we know today – no dishwasher, no carpeting, two bedrooms and one bath for six people, until I was 12. Our old dog Fuzzy, a Collie and Airedale mix, followed us to Dock #3 (then the loading dock for the Island) to catch the flashing yellow school bus on many a cold morning. The Point will always be an extraordinary place, even though many trees have fallen and more houses are being built all of the time. It was our place first when the school bus did not take the old road to Graham's Point at the end of State Street. Snowfall and road conditions in the winter, or about nine months of the year – the school year, – made that impossible. But General Delivery mail service rarely did not show up due to snow – some things we knew to always be true. The corner lot was our softball field with its cardboard make-shift bases and tree stumps for foul lines. The only house you saw on the East side of the Straits as you crossed the Bridge was our humble abode, the little one with the red roof just up from the Beach with that picture perfect view of the Bridge and the water flowing down Lake Michigan. Her ashes are buried there at the Point with a fountain and a garden just as she requested. We can always come home, come back to the Straits, to that place almost unchanged that will take us away from city life to a step back in time – to God's Country.

- ***She was the one who went away to college and supposedly returned with nothing.*** She never looked back, or did she? She had not taken her high school classes seriously, so college was not a stepping stone, it was a place where some of her friends were and where she wanted to be for awhile. I remember visiting her once at Central Michigan University (CMU) in Mt. Pleasant, while on my way back to Chicago and realizing instantly that she was a "short term student" and would be heading somewhere else soon to fly with her wings spread far. She was an artistic, creative and talented person and could easily have excelled in the home economics/dress design field that she thought she had chosen. Had she wanted it the way the school system says it should be for success, her days at (CMU) would have been quite different. Instead she took the unconventional route to personal success - the entrepreneurial, free spirit route. Later having a dress design and alterations business in her home fulfilled some of her dreams. In the eyes of her small close knit community, she was a successful person in her own right. Isn't that what is most important? Would a degree have altered her life drastically anyway, or made any difference? Could it have made her life fuller? Only she knows.

To stumble is normal.....brush off the dirt with the promise of God's forgiveness and move on.

Dr. Charles Swindoll

- *She was the rebellious one.* Rebellion is a two sided coin. It is usually used to describe the disruptive student, the indecisive free-spirit, the person going to jail, losing a corporate position or protesting a war when in fact it encompasses much more. My sister's rebellious nature was one of her more redeeming qualities. She epitomized taking the "road less traveled" and pursuing her loves. She made a place for herself by being her own person and not needing to have the latest fashions in the magazines. Her own look and panache was always appropriate. She showed her rebellious spirit by rebelling against convention and taking the old Oldsmobile Toronado out West one Fall to find her style, by rebelling against traditional ways and living with a man she hardly knew when it was not so fashionable, by being willing to leave him and plan to hike in Europe with another, and by abruptly transforming into a responsible adult when she learns she is going to have a child with an old friend. She was loved and respected for some of this, for the rest she just enjoyed her own comfort with her decisions. She was a big enough person to admit her errors before someone else exaggerated them. She knew when to "move on down the road."

- ***She was the compassionate one who made it warm and cozy to come home.*** "Home" was the "purple room" in the house on Church Street located across from the Catholic Church with its infamous holiday nativity scene. (The scene that her dogs inhabited when they wanted a warm spot out of the cold.) It was the home she decorated with her handmade beauties: the white crocheted afghan with the purple flowers that I've kept to this day; the vintage lace curtains; the lilac flower small print wallpaper with a contrasting and distinctive border; the antique brass beds and antique wood pieces in just the right places; the ceramic dolls that were hers and ones she "adopted" and dressed for others to enjoy; and the large and small bears that were hers and those rescued from thrift shops. The entire house had her distinctive taste, very European actually, with thrift shop and consignment treasures from clothing to furniture, from estate sales to a decorator's wallpaper. There were antiques from her husband's family, a family that has inhabited our hometown for over 150 years, plus nautical items such as lamps, tables and pen holders finished by our Dad of hardwood from shipwrecks on Lake Michigan. The wood "founded" (sank) when the big ships went down to rest at the bottom of the Great Lakes and then is rescued by divers to be used by craftsmen. The place was a statement of what she loved and acknowledged what we loved too. She took pride in Dad's craft and achievements, and decorated around these riches instead of using them to appease him until he was gone.

- ***She was the compassionate one that supported our Dad.*** She supported him through heart attacks, a stroke, hospitalization, and his passing. She tirelessly made trips with him 30-50 miles away, many times in the dead of winter in what we fondly referred to in the Upper Peninsula as "the tundra," to get him to his appointments. She helped Dad face the certainty of the situation, making decisions with him not to have heart surgery and to live with his failing health - difficult decisions on how to deal with a stroke, the partial paralysis and his possible recovery. She became his friend, no longer his foe. She was closer to him than any of the rest of us, and maybe always was because she was his namesake, the last one home and unexpectedly she was the first to go. She showed us that character is doing the right thing when no one is looking; we recognize she did more than we know and we are forever grateful to her.

- *She was the compassionate one that helped Mom cope with her Alzheimer's disease.* She helped Mom make major changes in her living situation when a strong person's help was needed. She did not complain or sing her own praises, she just did it. She did what needed to be done, and more. She knew it was what she could do, maybe had to do, but also wanted to do. She stepped up to the plate - she took the helm, and she showed us she was strong, not only our little sister anymore. She was not the one any of us would have picked for this job many years ago if that decision would have had to have been made earlier. She did not really know Mom and in many ways felt a void in that area, just as I did, until we realized Mom did the best she could for all of us. Mom lived in her own world most of her life and Alzheimer's seemed like the natural transition to her life. Our mother accepted the transition from independence in her own home to assisted living when my sister took her to a hospital for diagnosis; she accepted the situation's advancing stages when my sister had the responsibility of moving her from one level of care to the next, from group home to nursing home, to a Medicare facility and finally to rest peacefully in the Lakeside Cemetery. My sister seemed to intuitively know what to do and we were all so grateful. Hopefully those of us left behind said thanks more times than needed for all she did for our parents. Why do we wonder about those things long after someone is gone? Is it because we take things for granted or always feel there will be more time when we are ready?

- *She was also the compassionate one that became the executor of the estate.* She was the one that visited the nursing home when the rest of us were miles away, and the one that as executor had to take care of the expenses and rental of our family home, meeting the court dates and preparing for the audits. She did this without any credentials in property management or accounting, she did it on instinct, the way she functioned all of her life, the way it worked for her. She was the one making the decisions so that the care of Mom in our small hometown would be adequate and appropriate because these decisions had to be made. She was the one that bought Mom her clothes, such as special sweatshirts with flowers and animals on them. She was the one that bought her toiletries and made sure my high school friend, the best local hairdresser, came regularly to do Mom's hair. She was the one that talked about Mom's care to the nurses and the aides, many of them our high school friends; to be sure they understood our mother's needs. She was relentless in doing her duty, or

9

was it her pleasure to perform these functions? To have the responsibility of caring for someone who had tried to care for all of us, who had tried to do the best that she could, may have been a blessing in disguise for my sister. She had a chance I didn't to make it up to Mom for the many times we took her for granted. It is more rewarding to give than to receive was surely on her mind during those years.

• **She was the one that almost passed before the last parent.** Our mother had to pass after Dad; who would have cared for him so well? How would it have been for our parents watching their youngest daughter passing away before their eyes? They had to go in the order that God chose for them and for us. There is a plan. Our parents had her around long after the rest of us had gone; they had known her better than the rest of us because she was the last one. My Dad's early death from a multitude of heart problems many years earlier and my mother's death from Alzheimer's disease just the year before my sister's death had controlled the order of family loss anyway, especially since Alzheimer's had taken my Mom mentally five years before her actual demise. This was the way it was supposed to be. Yes, there is a plan, and my sister's departure after our parents passing was what they needed too. They needed her to take care of them in the end and to show all of us the gift of compassion. The rest of us will forever be asking "Could I have done that job and done it as well?"

• **She was the one we used to think needed to do more with her life.** She did not finish college, and as she once said "pissed away the last semester and now I am home." She did not pursue a traditional career, yet had a successful business of alterations and dress design in her home. Success is relative anyway, is it not? She did not get published, but continuously called the local St. Ignace Newspaper to correct grammar errors in its writing. She prided herself on these experiences. She had great taste and could mix and match the new with the old, trendy with vintage. She had her own expression and dared to show it everywhere such as in the clothing she sewed from scraps of velvet, fur and satin for donated antique dolls to be shown at Christmas time in our town's only department store, the front window at Winkelman's. Dolls that were later distributed to needy young girls in Mackinac County. She did more with her life than most and yet her life was cut in half when Cancer came to reign.

She gave me the gift of compassion.

I base most of my fashion taste on what doesn't itch!

Gilda Radner

Take time in the space provided to reflect on how compassionate you are and how you see compassion around you.

I think I need a hug....and a maid and a cook and a chauffeur and a secretary and an accountant.....and a lot more hugs.

Erma Bombeck

CHAPTER TWO
The Gift of Freedom

Our own individual faith in freedom can keep us free.

Dwight D. Eisenhower

High school was definitely different for her than me. I was an honor roll student with good grades, participating in many activities such as cheerleading, playing flute in the band, intra-mural volleyball, holding a class office, participating in drama club and getting crowned Carnival Queen for the band fundraiser.

I did these things because I wanted to do them, but also because they were expected of you at the time. I was the oldest of three daughters still at home and played that role with all its hope. I knew I was driven to succeed and liked the challenges and social interaction, the rewards and need for recognition. I was not ashamed of any of it, and she gave me the gift of freedom to be okay with those decisions.

I had a variety of boyfriends for proms and dances because that too was expected of high school girls in those days. High School in the 60's was changing from the style of the conservative 50's, but so much of the tradition was still incredibly important. Pushing the envelope, but not breaking too many rules, was as far as I could see myself going because old Dad was only going to tolerate so much. I had some freedom, and took a little more, but it took my little sister to teach me the true meaning of freedom.

Five years later, her years in high school in the 70's were crazy fun, many parties and silly pranks. The 70's were so carefree; they fit her well with lots of friends for great times and several handsome boyfriends to keep things interesting. She relished "getting by" with little studying and little valuing of a customary education. She always believed that life was to be lived your own way - that you had a right to freedom.

She realized early on that we have only one chance to pass this way and that life is to be lived daily. Her generation did not have a war; or losses by assassinations, as we did. They seemed free by their very status in life and she personified it. Her subconscious may have always known that her days were numbered; that her life would be cut shorter than ours and that living life to the very fullest was the only way she could do it. She broke a few more rules than me and pushed the envelope farther than I did, but no one was seriously hurt because her friendships survived and so did she – at least for awhile.

Dad said she gave him most of his gray hair, but that was always said with a smile. He mellowed a lot during her time in high school – living vicariously through her life and her friends. By the time she came along he was more laid-back since she was the last one of four daughters all together. He had spent a lot of energy on the rest of us, doing a good job of keeping us from drugs and unwanted pregnancies. He was tired and probably had decided to just watch the show.

She was not about to spend her high school years with her face in a textbook and miss out on the fun and the laughter. She was not about to be reined in by anyone and miss out on the chance to grab it all while it was there for the taking because she knew we pass this way only once and no one really knows what tomorrow will bring. She always seemed to have that insight when the rest of us seemed so

14

bogged down with thinking that we had to do so much, and all the time in the world to play later – never realizing that later may never come or come for only a short time.

Many time she would tell me to "lighten up" long before the phrase became trendy. Many times she would tell me to stop taking life so seriously long before I had read it over and over again in those books everyone said you had to read while maturing gracefully. She seemed to know what freedom was when really freedom had only been defined to us in government class our junior year. Our experiences with freedom had been so limited at this point – growing up in small town Americana, yet experimenting was what she did well and was willing to do, and so she taught me to taste freedom in many ways.

She taught me to look for ways to be free from someone's grip or my own mind's grasp and set myself free. We were both divorced very young for reasons we would not have anticipated would bring divorce and reasons we shared with each other.

She taught me to feel free even in the most confining situations, such as in the "job you love to hate" for it is not forever. So many times we had both worked those jobs to make ends meet when we so wanted to do what we loved or be somewhere else. She taught me to be free in mind and soul, and eventually the body would be free. "It would all work out" were exactly her words.

We both chose "doing our own thing" and being entrepreneurs as soon as that was possible, taking that leap to freedom. We both knew we were not really employees in the traditional sense. We realized that not being corporate material could be a noble thing and that having a home-based business and all the freedoms it entailed, long before it became the "thing-to-do," was giving yourself immense freedom - something else we were able to share early on in life.

The term "free spirit" defined her when we were not sure what a free spirit really was but thought it could be her. It was her karma, her destiny, and it was her gift to all of us. It was what we liked about her even when we could not be totally free ourselves at different times in our lives. It is one of my most cherished gifts from her.

She gave me the gift of freedom.

The cause of freedom is the cause of God.

William Lisle Blowles

Take time in the space provided to reflect on how freedom is working in your life or how it has eluded you.

I hate housework! You make the beds; you do the dishes and six months later
You have to start all over again.

Joan Rivers

CHAPTER THREE
The Gift of Friendship

God evidently does not intend us all to be rich or powerful, or great, but He does intend us all to be friends.

Ralph Waldo Emerson

After we were both divorced in the early 80's, I attended her 10th high school class reunion with her to share in the fun since she did not want to go alone. I was in town for my annual summer vacation so time was on my side. It was a funny idea to me that she would want my company while in the company of her friends she loved so dearly. She was never alone. She had a wealth of friends, guys and gals, her entire life. She finally talked me into attending even though it seemed so "juvenile" to go as sisters to a 10th class reunion. How grateful I am today for that time and appreciative of her friendship as well. I have wonderful memories of the evening, watching her entertain her classmates and share her wit, charm, love and friendship with them. She looked beautiful that night in a white cotton jumpsuit, belted by a raw silk deep purple colored sash, and of course with shoulder pads - so fitting of the 80's. Her hair was very long and curled slightly, that chestnut/dark auburn hair bouncing the way I want to remember it instead of the way Cancer made it, coarse and gray and unruly.

She enthusiastically received the "Miss Congeniality" award from her class, and I could see that her friends truly believed she should get this award. She played a big part in their lives. She was the mischief-maker with a good heart and a twinkle in her eye. She made them laugh and eventually, she made them cry; they knew she was truly a friend by her willingness to let them get to know her deeply. As expected, I first watched as an outsider that night as they danced and laughed together until I realized she and her friends were trying to include me. I was a part of what they were sharing with each other, even if it was just for one night. We all laughed and danced together, whirling around the room like spinning tops being free as we wanted to be, and kidded around with the teachers, just what she loved to do now that they saw her as an adult. They enjoyed her friendship too.

After the party that night, a group of us went down to the marina on the bay and slipped secretly onto someone's boat where we enjoyed good conversation, a lot of laughs and the excitement of knowing we were doing something we should not be doing, but not really causing any harm. The lake is so still, like a sheet of glass, on warm August nights in the Upper Peninsula. The Moran Bay inlet where the St. Ignace Marina lies in the heart of downtown, and now truly a focal point for visitors, has been expanded tremendously since that quiet night so long ago, but it will always be a place I'll remember from days gone by as a special place that holds a few secrets.

It's Friendship, Friendship – just a perfect Blendship.

Cole Porter

I continuously hear from several of her friends via email and regular mail while I make a point of seeing a couple of them when I am in Michigan. They share their friendship I am sure because I can represent her in some small way and they do not have to let her go completely. I share my friendship with them because they were a big part of her life, a comfort and joy to her, and I will always be grateful for what she had with that "sisterhood" as well. It served her well.

> *Treat your friends as you do your pictures,*
> *and place them in their best light.*
>
> ***Jennie Jerome Churchill***

She was truly blessed with faithful friends because she herself was a sincere friend. They showed our family during her time of illness how they could be true friends, even under the unhappiest circumstances. So many times they were available to comfort her and hold her, such as during the surprise-planning meeting for her last class reunion. It was held during that Christmas week we were all home at the big house where we were all congregated for a family reunion. Their coming together during that time of Chemo and baldness, fog and tiredness to include her in the planning by showing her they were there for her and that they needed her too, was a time to treasure.

I can still see them sitting around that large, antique dining room table, laughing and having fun as friends, the same as they had for decades. They brought their love and laughter and friendship to her that cold, crisp day in December during her remission by including her in planning their 25th class reunion some seven months before the occasion was to take place. She had no hair at the time, "bald as a baseball" with little energy, but a lot of hope. She gave them her friendship since that was all she had to give at the time, and they accepted it lovingly by making her feel important to the group.

Little did any of us know that this would be her last full and healthy summer with us, her last class reunion, her last time to see so many of those friends. None of them gave up on that friendship even when she was slipping away to a new place. Many times one of them would just stop by and sit with her while she slept, hold her hand, kiss her forehead or make her smile. Many of her friends brought food to the house time after time during her illness, doing many small things for her such as reading to her, helping her husband with a project or an errand, or taking time to talk to the boys. The small but precious gifts were not expected but always appreciated. They never saw it as a service or a duty, but as part of their friendship, and it showed.

Friendship is a sheltering tree;
oh, the joys that come down shower-like.

Samuel Taylor Coleridge

We both knew our friends know the worst about us, but refuse to believe it or remind us of anything negative. We had similar experiences with friends and knew their value as well as their necessity to be honest with us. She always believed friends forgive our shortcomings, and if very fond, they don't see any! She was right about that, and she valued what that meant with each and every one of them during those last days. Even the time they all assembled at her home on the Lake a year after the reunion to have a "dance" party with her only weeks before her passing. No matter how sick and weak and tired she was, they propped her up in a chair to be a part of the activities. They had asked her husband to leave, to be elsewhere, and they did not bring their husbands or wives, just their friendships as they laughed and joked and danced to '70's music the way they had 25 years earlier when life was simple and so full of wonder. No one wondered anymore – this was real life, no "70's story." The words were being written and they were willing to finish the story with her and not leave her to chance at the end of the road. Just one more reason why I will be forever grateful for their friendships, and what they did for her then and what they do now for her family. God bless them all.

She gave me the gift of friendship.

Blessed are they, who have the gift of making friends, for it is one of God's best gifts.

Thomas Hughes

Patricia L. Brooks

Take time in the space provided to reflect on the friendships you have made and kept and those you have lost or let go and how you feel about them today.

Friendships multiply joys and divide griefs.

Henry George Bohn

CHAPTER FOUR
The Gift of Love

This is the true measure of love; when we believe that we alone can love, that no one could ever have loved so before us, and that no one will ever love in the same way after us.

Johann Von Goethe

A relationship with a sister is like no other. It is not just the sibling rivalry or camaraderie; it is the supreme bond, a true sisterhood. It is a special kind of love and forgiveness, give and take and trial and error. It evolves and grows like so many other relationships, but it also has a special connection, a synergy, that makes life both bearable and magnificent.

It is those many heartfelt conversations with her before and after Cancer came into our family that have made my life broad and complete. We talked mostly by phone during those few short years before she passed, trying to live a lifetime in a short amount of space. We talked about everything and anything, usually how to transform our lives and make them healthier and happier, and what we were grateful for at the time. We tried to understand what happened when we were growing up, and how all of that – the good and the bad – impacted our lives. Why we had to have the Parents we did, and that we would have had it no other way was part of our conversation, and why both our parents had disappointed us some time along the way, and yet delighted us in their own way many times more. We both agreed: raising Parents is not easy!

Her Cancer gave me the guts to love being myself, to love my life just the way it was and to be able to be vulnerable

25

and confident with our relationship when I needed to be for her and for me. It gave me the guts to be willing to risk myself to be there for someone else, especially for her. It is a miracle that something so evil had a beautiful side, and that was the result of what happened to her and our family in our hearts, not what actually happened to her physical self. If she would have been in a car accident or had a heart attack, she could have been gone instantly. How much we would have all missed had she not slipped away slowly over those few years giving us all the chance to grow into ourselves and toward each other. As she would have said, "I faded into the sunset across the Lake, but I am still with you."

My sister's suffering, fighting and succumbing to Cancer taught me to:

- Live life fully each day.

- Keep life in perspective.

- Carry a positive attitude with me wherever I go.

- Take nothing for granted.

- Cherish the breath of life.

- Thank God for my health.

- Stop and smell the roses.

- Listen to the sounds of nature.

- Say please and thank you.

- Express love, but most importantly accept love.

- Allow someone to help me even when I cannot help myself.

- Be grateful for my life just the way it is.

- Not long for what is not God's plan for me.

- Let go of past fears and resentments.

- Smile.

I learned a long time ago when she faced divorce at a young age, and later in life quitting drinking – and staying quit, quitting smoking – and staying quit, that she relied on her love of life and her faith to sustain her. She knew when enough was enough and was able to see the big picture when that insight was so needed. She was also able to laugh at herself, love herself, and see the humor in being just like everyone else, or just a little more unique. She admitted her faults and shortcomings easily and moved on when it was necessary. She loved herself enough to love us and to allow us our shortcomings too. She had a capacity to love that included not being judgmental or critical. I will be forever appreciative of that quality. A quality found in the special few.

She never returned to smoking or alcohol after many, many years and especially not at the end when so many would have said, - "why not, what difference does it make?" It made a difference to her. It made a difference to how much she loved herself so she could love others.

I remember the day of her first surgery when I called her at the Mayo Clinic in Rochester. The front desk nurse put me through immediately which seemed strange to me. She had just left the recovery room after hours of exploratory surgery that left a large zigzag scar on her back. She learned that day that Cancer had come into her life, into our family. She told me immediately. I was speechless, then sympathetic, then comforting in some way, but definitely in disbelief. What did I think was wrong with her after six months of pneumonia and medications and ill health, after misdiagnosis and fatigue and lower back pain? Why was I in such denial about this situation? Had my subconscious just taken over and not allowed me to think the worst? I suppose it had, a survival technique I had used too many times in my life and one that was about to change forever.

She was not a "beat around the bush" type person. She always said what needed to be said, and said her piece when no one else would do it. She immediately began making decisions as to what she was willing to do to fight, because she had a loving husband and two boys in school, and they needed her desperately. She had to make decisions such as will I take Chemo, Radiation, have the lung removed, and agree to research, to interviews, and or to donating the lung.

This was my little sister, the rebellious one, but still the baby of the family, and not the one who was to go first. She was not the one who was supposed to make mature decisions that would impact all our lives, but she did so and I know she did it out of love. She did not tell any of us for over six months, until long after that first Christmas together, that the doctors at Mayo had given her six months to live. She waited to tell us, first, because it was too final and too soon, and second, because she was capable and willing to let us have our time to accept it all and to show her how much we loved her too.

Love is patient, love is kind…bears all things, hopes all things, endures all things. Love never fails.

The First Book of Corinthians

My sister's Cancer allows me to not take myself so seriously, but to take Cancer and my health seriously. She never saw me as a professional businesswoman with a good education and a successful career, not because she did not respect my decisions and admire my accomplishments, but because she was capable of loving me as more than that image. She understood those things, but I was still her sister who had made a lot of the same mistakes she had made. I was not going to be allowed to forget I too was from a small town in the Upper Peninsula of Michigan who just happens to have been a big city girl most of my adult life.

I truly believe Cancer is the great dividing wall of our generation. One in four people will get Cancer; it is more prevalent today than ever before for a lot of different reasons, some that cannot be explained. It is easy to justify why she would not be the one in four, but then it happens, and all the reasons why or why not do not matter. She had quit smoking 12 years before her diagnosis; she was not supposed to get lung Cancer. They, whoever they are, tell us that after 10 years without cigarettes your lungs are the same as they were before you started smoking. That is a lie, or certainly an unrealistic estimation of what is the truth of lung Cancer. The survival rate for women over 40 with lung Cancer is about 10%. She did not live in a big city with smog, air pollution, traffic and factories. She lived in small town Americana with no stop lights and a couple grocery stores; one high school where the sports team of that season is what happens in town, and where the local newspaper comes out every Thursday. It is a place where people who never leave home live out their lives and never regret it.

Why did this happen to her? She does not fit the profile, but she is the profile because Cancer does not discriminate. It will take any of us.

The anger eventually smolders somewhat and tackling the problem is what zaps your energy. She did not falter in taking her medications, in trying new holistic ideas and in being willing to learn about others who have survived and what they did. She never showed her anger outwardly although I saw it in her eyes many times; she just moved forward, sometimes slowly, sometimes with a chuckle and sometimes in silence, but always with love in her heart because she knew that even though this Cancer was her fight, we were all involved. She knew we could give the gift of love too.

Let love be your greatest aim.

The First Book of Corinthians

My sister's Cancer taught me to love and cherish the little things:

- *Take time for love and to enjoy the sunrise and the sunset.* She loved those glorious gifts of nature prevalent during cool spring mornings and warm summer nights at the Point on the Straits of Mackinac. She cherished this place where God put Lake Huron and Lake Michigan together to form a sanctuary like no other in the world. It was the place she chose to rest, the place where we grew up, the place we love and the place we will always call home. We thank God every time we see His grace and glory in the Straits of Mackinac that it even exists for us to yearn for one more summer.

- *Take time for love, to smell flowers and plant red geraniums on the patio.* Her favorite flowers always landed on the sun porch at the house on Church Street. Those lush red geraniums now surrounded the yard at the cottage on the Point like soldiers protecting her from anything harmful, only to surrender her at the end. She taught me to have a love of nature and natural things and not get caught up in what seems important at the time and not to confuse urgency with importance. She reminded me so many times in her weakening voice to not miss out on life's little pleasures like the "lilac store" across the Bridge in Mackinac City that has so much purple and lavender, the store that meant so much to her. She especially loved the lilacs and the Lilac Festival on the Island, one of those special events we shared as young girls and an event that continues even today - marking the entrance of "the good old summertime."

- *Take time for love and to enjoy children.* They were her treasures. She helped me realize that just because I did not bear children does not mean that I cannot be a special Aunt or Friend to her two boys. She gave me the good sense to start noticing other people's children and enjoying the children in our family, such as her own boys, my niece and my cousin's grandchildren.

- *Take time for love and to appreciate small creatures.* They were her pleasures. She made me realize, especially with her illness and our Mom's long suffering with Alzheimer's disease, that pets can play a great role in comforting the sick. Her three remaining Cocker Spaniels, Dylan, Bailey's Irish Cream and Patty McGee, were always at her feet and even at mine despite all the years I paid no attention to them, or even attempted to pet them. After she was gone and I was home that first summer, I tried to be a little more attentive to her

31

dogs. I knew they desperately missed her voice and her touch and that they were lost and heartbroken. The youngest, Bailey, died that summer shortly after we were all home for a reunion. Bailey needed to be with her and is now buried in the Garden by the Fountain, looking across Lake Huron where her spirit rests and her ashes lay. She had called Bailey home; he was her favorite.

- ***Take time for love and to read.*** It was her passion. She taught me to share acts of kindness that no one is aware of such as her reading to the children at the local library. It was not until the funeral that I learned there was a substantial fund at the library set up in her name, and that a memorial plaque would be done to say "thank you fine lady" for all your love and kindness to the children of this community. A "we appreciate you" memorial plaque for the many occasions she read unselfishly to the children, long after her boys had outgrown their days of her reading to them. The plaque has a place in the new library which will be constructed soon, another symbol of her spirit kept alive and her gift of love made visible. Quiet time at the library has become even more of a haven for me, a place of joy and comfort, and a time to celebrate my sister again.

- ***Take time for love and to cherish old songs.*** They were her joy. She was the Queen of 70's trivia, of 70's tunes and singers. She loved being the one to have the answer and maybe even the record or tape at the time. She loved that look and that era of "no war" and fun and silliness. She liked the naïve aspect of the era too, even though she was far from naïve. Life had been too real early on in her life,

32

like it is for many of us. She was nobody's fool, but loved to play the fool. She epitomized the 70's and was proud of it; she kept the memories alive in so many songs, stories and photos of her and her friends, planning her class reunion every five years and always valuing friendships by keeping in touch.

- ***Take time for love and to laugh, and to tell and appreciate a good joke.*** That was a big part of her sense of humor. I still can't tell jokes, and she would be the first to correct my joke telling or remember the punch line for me, but I know to appreciate good jokes and the people that bring humor into our lives. She is gone, but the special person that has come into my life since her passing has that sense of humor and quick wit. She would have enjoyed bantering and joke telling with him. He is a gift to continue the jokes when we think it is even the worst of times. Whenever I think of her, I smile inside and out.

- ***Take time for love and to visit special places.*** They were her fantasy. She longed to travel and talked more and more of venturing to Ireland and to leaving her spirit there, but it was not meant to be until I visited Ireland to fulfill her dream. I clearly remember the year she called and asked if she could come and live with me for the winter. I agreed since I was living alone in a two-bedroom townhouse in Arizona and knew she needed to get out of the harsh winters of Northern Michigan. She was to make the trip in her old Toronado with one of her dear friends, but they did not make it and ended up in Colorado. The car would not go any farther. It was an adventurous trip that ended with her staying there for about a year to earn a living and change the course of her life forever. She made the best of a not so perfect situation, but that was as far as she was to go since the events from that point forward shaped her life. They were a short relationship, a dead-end job, a cancelled trip to hike across Europe, and a new life as wife and mother. This turn around could not have happened faster and the course of events more planned if she had written the script herself, instead of letting God's plan unfold before her.

If we give someone a piece of bread and butter, that's kindness, but if we put jelly or peanut butter on it, then it's loving kindness.

Barbara Johnson

I know I have to live for both of us because she had a lot of living left to do, lives to touch and great things to challenge. This life of mine is not just for me anymore. I feel motivated to: take action on things I have been ignoring; work on things that I love without the thought of monetary gain; do "what I love" and let the money or success in any form follow; and honor and cherish that special person who came into my life shortly after her passing. She would have loved him too.

Ironically, the summer she was in remission, her high school class had their 25th reunion and my high school class had its 30th reunion on the same beautiful day in July in our hometown. It was a sun filled and warm week with a chance to wear a strapless dress and feel comfortable for that short time in August when even Northern Michigan is busting with summertime. The days were full of events such as the infamous bonfire on the Lake at her home. Her friends and mine shared in their class reunion memories and reminisced about the way it was in 1968 and 1973. Everyone stayed way past midnight when only the embers of the fire threw light on the Lake. No one left until he or she was ready to leave; everyone was welcome for as long as they wished; it was a happy occasion in a sequence of unhappy moments.

I was to emcee my 30th reunion that year, as I had for the 10th and the 20th. Those times were happier times when I had written and presented humorous and memorable talks. This time was different, I had done research and had written something, but it was too serious and would not compare to times gone by. I was unprepared the night of the reunion parties because I threw out what I had written. I knew I had to relish the opportunity to be free to handle this night any way I wanted to handle it. She understood; she had been watching me get dressed, do my hair and try to prepare for the emcee part of the night. She had been at my 20th as the bartender and had heard my "stand up routine" at a time in our lives when things were really very good. We now knew it not to be true.

Everyone knew she had been ill and hopefully understood, but they did not need to understand. There is a great freedom in knowing at times that you can do what is right for you, and it is okay with God, and most of the rest of the world. I did a short presentation when introduced and allowed myself to not be in the limelight that evening.

I had the most fun that night ending the evening at her reunion party with her husband and her friends just down the street at a local club, taking some of my friends with me to her party. There is something special about small town Americana and class reunions in the summertime that cannot be duplicated. It is a time of romance and laughter, tears and reminiscing, and sadness and loss for a time gone by. It is a time to be ourselves no matter who we are because we are home and we are in the comfort of home. We are one again.

It took me a long time to accept the reality of these circumstances, to believe that she really was going to pass away from us and that this was God's plan. That God loved her and her family, all of us, and that it was not our place to ask why. Life will happen; there is a plan for all of us. To love God unconditionally was truly a test for me at this time. I fought it harder at the end than in the beginning, when my faith was truly being tested, when I had to soul search and find my most intimate feelings about life's inequities. I have since come to peace with most of it. My love of God is restored and it is only because of her love for all of us and her love of God that I was able to do this.

She gave me the gift of love.

Love each other…..and take delight in honoring each other.

The Book of Romans

Take time in the space provided to reflect on how you express love and how love is given to you.

Time is a dressmaker specializing in alterations.

Faith Baldwin

CHAPTER FIVE
The Gift of Contentment

The contented spirit is the sweetness of existence.

Charles Dickens

The Thanksgiving she was in remission she came to visit me for a week here in Arizona, a long trip from Northern Michigan and the life she knew so well. She came alone since her husband and boys were going to a family deer hunting camp - their usual mode of operation for this time of the year that they continue doing even today. This was usually her Christmas shopping time in a nearby city with her close friends: it was a big event in their lives since they spent the night in that city to have a two-day marathon of "shop 'til you drop", something that had been a tradition for them for a long time. But we knew this year was to be different and special for us, with some shopping but certainly a lot of sharing and experiencing our relationship in a way we had never allowed to happen. We knew when it was just the two of us, we would have time to talk and express our thoughts. This was something we both loved to do and knew we needed to do because life had become so precious so quickly.

Pleasant words are a honeycomb,
sweet to the soul and healing.

The Book of Proverbs

She came to see me at this time because she had always wanted to visit again without her husband or her boys, so the two of us could have our time, to recapture some moments we had taken for granted when we were younger and home in Michigan. She came to try to recall a time that may have been taken from us before it could be cherished. She came for me as much as for her; because she knew I was not at peace, and that contentment had eluded me many times and was not our friend now either.

Our time together was spent horseback riding in a desert and mountainous park, high above the city, with a "blue eyed" cowboy just ornery enough to make her laugh and quip along with him. As she would say again and again, "my kind of guy" - while trying to convince me I should give him my phone number! She always thought she was looking out for me. The two-hour ride was peaceful and uneventful, but I could tell it meant so much to her. It gave her contentment.

One day that week was also spent at the Phoenix Zoo, taking much needed time to pet the small furry goats and lambs in the children's zoo as well as enjoying the wonder of the larger animals such as the lion and the elephant. She was at home with animals and at home in this environment, content with the simplicity of a day at the Zoo. At times that day she struggled with walking up slight hills, but she did not quit because it was going to be memorable. She was determined to make the best of the situation; she had learned to do that so well in life and especially in the last couple of years. She was not going to let that wicked Cancer rule. Thank-you God for that special place.

Our time was also spent going out to lunch, being free to talk about her surgeries and how she felt with a body part missing. The space in the cavity in her chest that had held her lung was the topic of conversation. She seemed content with that loss and talking about it where I was amazed and curious. She told me the space fills with a substance like jell-o and that the rest of the body adapts. I suppose like we do, the body becomes somewhat content again and adjusts to its new shape or course. The body is an amazing piece of machinery, and we should acknowledge that and only hope and pray for good working order for all of us. We were content in knowing God had a plan and He was there for us then and He is there for us now.

Our time was spent as well as with my women friends. Friendships with women were important to her and I wanted to show her they are to me too. We met my friends for lunch the last day of her vacation at a great southwestern restaurant, something she could only experience in this area. We took pictures in the outdoor mall with its specialty shops and lush plants; it was being decorated for the holidays and the poinsettias were a perfect backdrop for our pictures because they were being used to build holiday trees. We had dressed for the occasion in black and leopard prints, and we felt good. She enjoyed listening to our conversations which I am sure many times were new topics to her. She hadn't been single for a long time, or lived alone for much of her life; all of us had done those things repeatedly. She had not had a career outside the home like we did, but her own business in the home, so our experiences in a working day were very different, especially living in a large city.

Our lives appeared so different on the outside, but were so much the same on the inside. She was my sister, for sure, but my friend for eternity. We knew we were bonded for life's events and by our souls and experiences. She knew I felt her pain because this could have been me just as easily. We had the same genes and believed so much of what life has in store for us is genetic first and life second.

Patricia L. Brooks

No one has greater love than this,
to lay down one's life for one's friends.

The Book of John

We were invited to a friend's home for Thanksgiving dinner and it proved to be a meaningful time as I suspected it would. She was a friend I knew I could count on in this time of need. She was like my sister in a lot of ways and that made it fun for all of us.

My sister and I knew we were seeing her two boys' years down the road, ready to graduate from college, as we looked across the table at my friend's boys only a few years older than my nephews - nice boys, handsome, well-behaved, bright, and loving their mother. My sister knew that feeling of completeness and what that feeling meant; how it had sustained her through all those terrible months. We assembled there for a lovely Thanksgiving dinner, the five of us. My friend's home, and traditional Thanksgiving setting in the dining room, were so like my sister that we felt at home and a part of the "family" in this most precarious situation.

A great cook lives in this wonderful house. A former Home Economics major just like my sister, a "crafty" and creative person in a quaint French country style home with wooden shutters and flowerpots, large fruit trees and a plant garden window-box. The kitchen, in an eclectic style, was perfect for all of us with its many tasty smells and tantalizing scents. Outdoors more great scents abounded with a lush and plentiful garden of vegetables, flowers, and herbs – all those things that tell you this is a home filled with love and tender loving care. The event was topped off with a new Cocker Spaniel puppy – nothing could have been more perfect. My sister's three Cocker Spaniels were the loves of her life. The setting was exceptional; she was at home and in a place she felt safe. I could see the contentment on her face.

I once asked a small child what he thought a home was and he replied.
"It's a place to come in out of the rain."

Gigi Graham Zchividjan

What a poignant moment a year later when I had Thanksgiving dinner with the same friend, her sons and a few others. How hard it was to be there without my sister and to smile and go on when I did not want to go on anywhere. My sister's physical presence was not there, she had passed that previous August, but she was there in spirit and we all knew it. My friend's two boys are two years apart like my sister's boys, but several years older. Many times that day I saw my nephews in her boys and knew they would be okay, just as my nephews would be okay, because these boys too are shaping into productive and impressive young men. God takes care of children, young and old, and he will take care of all of them too – and for this I find contentment.

She gave me the gift of contentment.

True contentment is getting out of any situation all that there is in it.

Gilbert Keith Chesterton

Take time in the space provided to reflect on how content you are today and how content you want to be in the future.

Content makes poor men rich;
discontent makes rich men poor.

Benjamin Franklin

CHAPTER SIX
The Gift of Tolerance

*Tolerance is giving to every other human being
every right that you claim for yourself.*

Robert G. Ingersoll

I was there for only a short week with her that last summer, which began with my being mostly alone with her and her disease at a small, but quaint, beachfront property overlooking the Bay and the Island, the place she had decorated so well for summer visitors who came through each year, some becoming friends. The Ferry Boats were clearly in sight out the large windows that framed their crossing to the Island making their fantail waves as they cut through the beautiful blue waters every few minutes just as they had 30 years ago when we were all home and life was simple. Our view off the redwood deck and from the large living room window captured a moment in time I will always treasure. The neighbor's home was a showplace of flowers and layers of green and lushness, the "award winner" of the town, as it was every summer. It all seemed so small town picture perfect, so Norman Rockwell, so Alistair Cooke, just for a moment.

The fantail wave at the back of the Ferry Boat and the sound of the boat's foghorn as it left the shoreline of the Bay were so familiar and comforting as I sat alone on the large freshly-stained, redwood deck outside the rear of the house. The summer place was ready for guests and happier times. My sister was asleep in the front bedroom in that Chemo stupor that lasts several days. We were away from her permanent home down the turn at the Point, but nearby in a

45

place that gave us some privacy and quiet time to hopefully help her relax and get through another one of her "sessions." It was a place she had proudly decorated for summer visitors just one year earlier, and now we were the visitors. How strange that must have been for her, or maybe she did not notice since she had more important things to contemplate, such as tolerating a terminal disease and all that entails. She was always so involved and busy with creating special places such as this space; now all of that was being taken away and each day was a challenge just to breathe and sleep and eat and keep going.

The look on her face during this time was so distant, sad and longing for days gone by. I could see she was just trying to cope with each small effort she made and that my being there helped, but only made a slight difference. There were times when she was alone with God and her disease, and no one or nothing else could change that situation.

Her husband suggested we stay here at "the rental," as it was called, because the next tenants were not due for a week. It was almost August, the height of the season and time to make good rents on this place. He knew she needed a change of scenery, a different view of the vastness of the Great Lakes and the sounds of life on the water since their home at the Point was crowded and busy. She had taught all of us tolerance during these times of inconvenience, but there was a limit and it was time to do more for her.

Be patient enough to live one day at a time as God taught us, letting yesterday go and leaving tomorrow till it arrives.

John E. Newton

Their boys had a lot of friends and activities, and seemed oblivious sometimes to what was really happening.

I know it was their way of coping with the unknown and the terrifying truth of Cancer and what it can do. They loved their mother deeply, but this was their early teen years and they had their own way of showing their love for her and understanding the horrible truth of this reality. They had their own level of tolerance. They were trying to keep things the same and discover ways to tolerate the most disgusting of circumstances. They were desperately trying to do it their own way. They were still children. Tolerating the unacceptable was not yet in their realm, but their mother was demonstrating commitment and sacrifice to them and to all of us everyday.

I took her to the small emergency room (ER) twice in those first four days of my vacation, two times too many for anyone. We went to the Mackinac Straits Hospital in our hometown, the same hospital that was new to the community when she was born in 1955, only to be greeted by people we had known for a lifetime. The hospital that now seemed so small and ill-equipped to deal with such an overwhelming task of seeing her through these days.

She was incoherent and dehydrated, attempting to give me instructions on how to get there and where to park in a voice I could not recognize or understand. It was raining, chilly and damp, and I had a hard time taking care of her as we struggled to get from the car to the emergency room door. I had brought a blanket to cover her, but nothing felt like it was working, everything was amiss. She had shown me where to park until I realized she was not herself and that we were a long way from the (ER). That action was so foreign to me; I was used to her being in charge when I was home again. Now I was making it up as I went along, hoping I never had to pass this way again.

Sometimes it felt like she was already gone to a world we can only imagine. She was slowly becoming a shell and I so desperately wanted her back again. It was eerie taking her to the local hospital; it seemed so small in size compared to what I remembered as a young girl. The hospital staff was waiting for her at the (ER) door, and knew what to do. They had been down this road before, with her and many others. Cancer impacts one in four lives, even in small town Americana, and most of the time with no explanation. We tolerate the situation and pact with it as best we can. She had her pact with God and succumbed to the treatment they administered, tolerating their every move as if she could live outside what was happening. Sometimes I felt like she could have survived war imprisonment just as easily as she had built up such a tolerance for the cruelty of this prison.

Earlier that morning, I had been baking chocolate chip cookies at the main house down State Street at the Straits of Mackinac watching the cars cross the Bridge. I was desperately trying to give her boys some sense of normalcy with homemade cookies when really I was hiding out in "the way it used to be," and the familiarity of her little old kitchen with the red and white knick-knacks everywhere and Mom's old red "swag" lamp hanging over the counter. The knotty pine walls watched me in the "cabin" as I worked. It was raining with just a chill in the air. I was not ready to tolerate a situation that you cannot prepare for in life. I like a "heads-up" in everything and a chance to prepare so I will make minimal mistakes; this was not one of those times. Cancer does not come with warnings – it is the silent killer. Cancer does not give those of us who have to have organization to our lives any time to "get ready," to prepare, to organize. My tolerance of this reality was being tested every minute. Nothing came in the way I wanted it to come in, and it surely left as it pleased.

Look for a long time at what pleases you, and longer still at what pains you.

Collette

As I watched the constant rain coming down on the lush green grass that needed to be mowed and those deep red Geraniums smiling brightly from many flowerpots next to the old storage shed and the shoreline, her three Cocker Spaniels slept contentedly in their old worn beds. I kept thinking "how did we get here" from there and where did all the flowers go, the daisies and forget-me-nots that used to be everywhere at the Point? Those were the flowers of childhood that represent innocence to me even today, with hope and new beginnings.

How did we get away from those trips to the Island, the smell of horse manure in a place with no cars? ...... missing as well the smell of Mackinac Island fudge almost too sweet, but so important to the memories.

Where did the time go to take those outings at the Sand Dunes with high-rolling, foaming swells in Lake Michigan to tackle if you dared? ......those times when you knew why you loved summers in this part of the North Country......those chances to ride horses from the old stables across from the Dunes with not only those high-rolling swells, but the fresh wet air in your face.

Where was the much needed time to stop for Pasties at Lehto's old roadside stand coming home on US 2 West? ......those flaky dough "hot meals" of potato, some vegetables and maybe meat cubes that you can get nowhere else......those "delights" of childhood my Jewish friends here in the city call knish.

How did we get away from having breakfast as a family at the Galley, where no cappuccinos are served, yet ketchup is always on the table? ......forgetting the rule you only eat bacon on vacation because it isn't good for you... ....enjoying the Big C burger at Clyde's, large and juicy and made the same way it was made in 1965......taking trips to Glen's grocery to plan for a cookout in the backyard with that old stone fireplace and weathered griddle Dad made from large rock off the causeway near the Bridge when we were very young girls.

He knew it would be a place we would still call home, where life would remain pretty much the same for decades, the way it is supposed to be and where we could always go home. Before Dad's heart attack, Mom's Alzheimer's and Cancer in my sister's lung made God's Country a test of patience and tolerance, we had it all and we were having a hard time now tolerating anything less.

Who decides when it needs to change, when we need to tolerate the unthinkable, and when tolerance is now a family pastime? Change is inevitable, it is life and it comes at us in big pieces and little pieces. Sometimes we do not welcome change and other times we seek it out. At times it may be an inequity of life, but it is ever present just the same. For me these changes were excruciatingly painful, intolerable in a situation you had to tolerate for her and she showed you how to do it.

She was coming off the Chemo from the week before when I took her into the (ER), and she was not coherent or any where close to herself. She wasn't quick-witted and full of stories and jokes. She was in that "fog" that eventually lifts only after saline is put in through IV's, and there is rest and some time on her side. This was my first experience with this (ER) place with all its "sickness" and stainless steel and sterility and pungent cleaning product smells. I did not like this place at all, but tolerating it was what had to be done. Frankly, I distained it and tried desperately not to show my disdain. It seemed void of anything warm and fuzzy. It was bleak at best, not at all the way my sister liked her surroundings. Nothing had color or texture or cheer, not the workers, not the walls in her room or the hallways surrounding them. This was not about me anyway, and it never was, it was all about her and I cherish this time I had to give of myself in any small way. Thank God, I did not miss this chance

One of her friends from high school, who now worked at the hospital, met us there. She seemed displaced and my sister seemed uninterested in her or who was there. This friend had brought a small plastic bottle of "blessed oil" from a particular place in Canada where Catholic priests live and bless this oil. It was to comfort her and help her with the skin problems that come with Chemo and Cancer. Her friend presented it in a very uncomfortable way, not giving it or my sister the value they probably deserved; she must not have known how to do this, if there is a right way. She was ill-prepared to see her old friend in such a condition. She had not yet learned the tolerance game. The "life of the party" had the lights down low and this friend was lost in the dark. The emptiness of that situation is haunting to me even now.

I don't want to get to the end of my life and find that I just lived the length of it.
I want to have lived the width of it as well.

Diane Ackerman

At this point my sister could not keep down any of the medications, 15-20 pills that she was expected to withstand daily. She could barely eat; her swallow mechanism was not working properly, not even a Hershey bar or a Coke, two of her favorites, went down easily or even appealed to her. Her husband told me I had to make her bear the pills – she had to take them, but I could not do that, it seemed so cruel and inhumane. Persistence could not apply here; it just did not seem to fit. This was not a competition; this was not a race to the end. I was not equipped to do any of this, but somehow found myself doing the best I could.

I think of myself as an accepting and tolerant person, but I had met my match with this disease. I was at a low tolerance level for any new challenge, especially in the category of caregiver, and I knew it. My own headaches had kicked in and I was vomiting from all the stress that surrounded us. I found myself nursing her when I felt sickened, not with her but with this Cancer and what it had done to this beautiful person. It was so unfair to see her declining; she deserved so much more. She deserved everything. My concept of patience and tolerance had now taken on a whole new meaning. I was grappling with the idea of taking charge but there was nothing to take charge of here; tolerance was the order of the day and I had to muster up any form of acceptance I had ever learned.

I woke her that final morning at the end of my vacation week, the morning I had scheduled to go home to Arizona, fearing and knowing in my heart it could be the last time I would see her alive.

What made me feel that in my gut?

What possessed me to insist on seeing her one more time before heading to the airport?

I was staying at our family homestead up the road and remember that last surreal walk down toward the Lake and through the trail in the woods to her new place of residence – a walk we had taken many times as kids as we headed to the Lake for a swim. It had always been a glorious walk that had meant fun, surprise and excitement, not pain and suffering, sadness and good-bye forever.

Her husband and the boys were up and stirring, trying to do the so called "normal things" you do before taking a day trip such as cleaning up the kitchen, packing the cooler with soft drinks and snacks, as well as packing blankets and pillows, games and magazines in the back of the vehicle.

The small iron bed where she lay in the loft seemed cluttered but cozy, her stuffed animals nearby and several half read small books stacked nearby as well. The stench of sickness permeated the loft even though the windows on the Lake side of the house were slightly ajar and the freshness of a summer morning in Northern Michigan could be sensed like an early morning shower. It was just the way she always liked things, comfortable, cool and just a little chaotic.

The sun was peeking through the half opened window while throwing a glistening trail across the Lake, its color a pale orange, getting brighter ever so slightly. Her things were nearby, all those bottles of pills, a glass of water, a book of aspirations and a picture of the boys when they were younger. I woke her and told her it was time to get dressed. She did not answer but the look of sadness on her face told the story. She was way ahead of all of us; she knew more poison was in store, and she knew it was futile. I think she had been talking to God about his plan for a long time. She knew God was going to stop the trying and turn her down the road of acceptance very soon. We knew it too; we just had to verbalize it somehow.

She was so pale and thin, not at all the way I will remember, helping her dress was extremely difficult. No more rosy cheeks and sparkling eyes, no more wide toothy grin and glossy chestnut hair. That was then, and now that she is in a better place, I can remember just exactly what I want to remember. None of her clothes fit at that point, she was thinner than me for the first time in 20 years. She was so weak and disoriented; God had already taken her "earthly" independence and replaced it with a patience and tolerance I could only hope to know in my lifetime. I knew she would be making no decisions for herself that morning, and that scared me. She was getting more ill and vomiting uncontrollably as the morning wore on, her body preparing for the poison. Her body knew more than the doctors and certainly knew when it was time for the poison. Her body knew that more Chemo was not going to make any difference, that it was time to stop and the vomiting was its way of telling us so.

Why do humans listen less to their own bodies and the bodies of others than they do to the engine in their car? The tolerance expected of a Cancer patient with regards to Chemo and Radiation is more than I can comprehend. It is patience and tolerance far greater than anyone should have to endure. The poison process is so antiquated at best and needs to be improved now. God help those who are trying to make that happen.

We no longer use bloodsuckers to heal, why do we continue to use the "poison" of Chemo? This is a disease of huge proportions and must be eradicated, if for no other reason than to do away with the shear cruelness of this inhumane treatment to men, women and children.

Each time she was due for a Chemo appointment her body revolted, either warning of what was to come or calling for more of that poison as if it was an addiction and she needed it to keep going. The Chemo had a mind of its own. The anger about this treatment was present with all of us, but in a different form. We all knew it was archaic and futile, but we did not know what else to do or where to go for more hope or more help, or how to stop it or what to say to make it better or when to change things. We were paralyzed with procedure as if in a cage peering out at this point to a life and a family that was out of reach for any of us, especially her and her needs.

I vocalized my true feelings later to my other sister and her family, after that heart- wrenching good-bye. That good-bye where she begged me not to get on the plane, but to get in the vehicle with her and stay forever, which may have only been a few weeks. That good-bye where she tried to hug me back but no strength was available to her. She was frail, and weak, and not herself in too many ways.

The other family members were driving me some 30 miles to the little airport in Pellston for a ride again on the prop to Detroit. I would then return home to Phoenix on the other side of the country. I knew I would never see my younger sister again, that this was the end. That sad, heavy and sinking feeling I had was a feeling like no other, but maybe close to how I would feel falling into a pit by accident as the natural light disappeared. There was a silence in the car, my other sister and her husband and daughter knew I was right and they could not respond, either it was physically or emotionally impossible or it was both. None of us wanted to think about how different life would be soon. How sometime soon one of the beacons of light in the window on the Beach would go out forever.

To know that in the storms to come, one light would not shine brightly, or would it? The light we give to others shines long after we are gone; we impact people far greater than we know. This is certainly true for my sister, her light shines ever so brightly. Too many times I have heard a person say kind and loving things about someone who has passed, knowing full well they did not vocalize that kind of love to that person when that person walked amongst us. They did not tolerate the little idiosyncrasies of that person when he or she was alive only to find they desperately want to remember the idiosyncrasies after the person is gone. We were not going to let that happen. I knew I could not live with myself if I did not say I love you with a kiss one more time, if I did not tolerate everything about this situation and make the best of it.

She gave me the gift of tolerance.

In everything give thanks.

The First Book of Thessalonians

Take time in the space provided to reflect on how tolerant you are in situations that cause you pain or anger.

For fast acting relief, try slowing down.

Lily Tomlin

CHAPTER SEVEN
The Gift of Hope

Hope is the thing with feathers that perches in the soul.

Emily Dickinson

The first Christmas she was ill we had a large family reunion, 13 in all came together willingly as a time to be with her and family. We met at her husband's large 100-year- old family home, the one with six bedrooms (including a Murphy bed) and eight bathrooms, with additional room heaters everywhere to help brace the winter cold. The frontal view of the house delivers six large white pillars that call you to the front door because they are so curious and representative of a time gone by, a replica of the feelings we all had and were afraid to acknowledge. The home also had an extended wooden porch around three-quarters of the house, holding all of us in its arms because we needed that so badly. The corner lot, located in the heart of our hometown, seems perfect to display this historical site that maybe someday will be open for all in the community to see.

It has a charming dining room that could easily seat all 13 of us as we dined together and desperately worked to make this house feel like our home for the week. The house also showed off an ornately wallpapered piano room complete with a baby grand and overly done velvet drapes, thus the perfect spot for the infamous family picture. We were in our best with my sister perched appropriately in the front of the group in her black velvet dress and hat, bearing an antique broach - she was eloquent for delayed timing of the camera on the tri-pod.

The parlor at the front of the house held several wood claw chairs and loveseats, and of course, the beautifully decorated Christmas tree - just the way the tree in the story of *Little Women* was portrayed. It was an authentic holiday tree with no store bought ornaments or tinsel, in a room with no TV or stereo or video games, just warmth and quiet and sleeping cats on the old maroon velvet winged back loveseat.

Remnants of the stable and barn are still out back, just as they were 100 years ago. The house is close enough to downtown and just up the street from the Bay and Marina that overlook the Island, a block from the Catholic Church that houses a lifetime of memories for all of us. It was about as Norman Rockwell as we could get, and we enjoyed ourselves immensely despite the odds, actually feeling that things were somewhat normal when we all sat down together for breakfast or a competitive game of Scrabble.

It was a grand time, but like all family reunions it was not without its flawed moments and missed opportunities to get to know each other even better. We did not talk enough about the "evil" living amongst us. We were all living with Cancer at that point, and fighting our own battle with immortality that had always seemed destined for the older ones in the family and not for the "baby boomer" generation of the family.

My sister had just lost her beautiful, chestnut-brown hair so we were all getting used to this display of Cancer's reality. Baldness can be the "ugly" side of Cancer, but she would not allow it to be and forced us to see her as just as cute without hair as she was with that long bouncing hair of our youth. She was also healing from a large incision to the back. The incision where they went in to "explore" the situation and determine, unbeknown to us at the time, that she had six months to live. She kept that from us for the duration, trying to protect us, trying to be the strong one. My little sister who had carried the load so many times with caring for our parents was still trying to do that for us. Who knew she would be the stronger one? She never gave up hope and never wanted to take hope away from any of us.

Sometimes I would catch her sitting to the side listening to the conversations we would have at the kitchen table in that big country kitchen, taking it all in, almost as if she was removed from us in someway. Almost as if she was in a different place we could only imagine. This was a new Sister, not the one we grew up with, not the one who was always the center of attention because of her wit and jokes and laughter, not the one who came last in line and first in Dad's heart - she was different now and changed forever because Cancer came into her life and took something away that would not come back, even though she made sure it did not take hope.

A light heart lives long.

Shakespeare

She was so brave to choose life without a wig and wear hats of all shapes and sizes, and bandanas the same way she did so often in the summer when donning a pair of cut-off jeans and a tank top that made a statement only she would dare make. She always loved her hair short, extremely short and was not defined by hair or makeup, but by the cherub look, freckles and a great smile. I kept the hat I purchased for her that year, black velvet with a brim, a special adjustable strap inside to fit a head with no hair, a head that was different only on the outside. It was so perfect for the rhinestone broche she loved to wear. I have her broche and will keep it forever. The blue stones especially, remind me of her. She wore that specially made black velvet hat on Christmas Eve that year, looking impressive and stylish even in her condition because there was hope in her heart and faith in her soul. We all benefited from that strength and gift of hope, and I am sure always will.

I have since, by accident, misplaced that hat on a trip and know I will never see it again. I have had to forgive myself for my carelessness and believe that the person now wearing it will enjoy it. I miss that hat, I liked wearing it and that feeling I had that my sister was still with me. Please God, allow the new owner of the hat hope too.

We walked that Christmas Eve night in a light dusting of freshly fallen snow just a couple blocks to the corner to attend Catholic Mass. The old town church was the same in many ways, larger than some memories and certainly older, and so traditional. Our hometown is over 340 years old, founded by Father Marquette and the French, and this church reflects so much of that history. I remembered it as very traditional and not like the church I attend in Arizona, the one with musical instruments and casual dress, and friars in sandals. So many familiar faces I could not name that night as we walked down the long aisle to communion, but I knew they all knew her and had her in their prayers with a hope that this too would pass. She had made an impact on this community and they were not going to forget her or let her go easily; they were hopeful for even a few more months for her.

We opened our Christmas gifts together the next morning in the front parlor near that beautiful tree. Snow had fallen in the night and a fresh glittering layer was on the window sill outside encircling what was hopefully a precious moment for all of us. We enjoyed the surprise inside the package just the way we did when we were little girls in that town anticipating a new snow and our new winterized gifts - usually gifts of new flannel nightgowns, gloves, hats and scarves, but sometimes as it was this time, more memorable items like books or special jewelry.

But the true gift that morning that filled our hearts was we still had hope because she had kept the hope alive even though she was dealing with the secret "it" was terminal. She did not accept the doctors at Mayo saying she had six months to live; she had things to do and people to love before she left this earth behind. They told her to take a trip to Hawaii or wherever she had always wanted to go, and she chose home and us. They told her to go and do whatever she had always wanted to do, and she chose loving her family and giving hope. She knew she was a fighter and that she would do whatever it took to buy some time to be all she could be for us, to give the gift of hope and not desperation, and to love more before it was time to say goodbye.

She gave me the gift of hope.

Hope does not depend on having a blue print for the future.

Rebecca Manley Pippert

Take time in the space provided to reflect on what you hope for this year and if you have lost hope in any area.

There is no medicine like hope, no incentive so great, and no tonic so powerful as expectation of something better tomorrow.

Orison Swett Marden

CHAPTER EIGHT
The Gift of Patience

Adopt the pace of nature; her secret is patience.

Ralph Waldo Emerson

She passed away about six weeks after I was home that last summer. The family, including myself, tried desperately that last week we were all together to have some semblance of normal life, yet never forgetting what was so apparent. We attended the 4th of July parade down State Street with all its hometown flavor of marching veterans and children in clown suits with decorated bicycles, with floats representing local businesses and organizations and of course, high school alumni make-shift bands on flat-bed trucks. For only fleeting moments, life was the way it always was and it was fun again.

We all wanted to participate in the celebration activities as much as possible because we knew that was what she wanted for us, and that we needed to live life, be patient and wait for signs from God that things would change again.

We included in the week such events as the Kiwanis Club cookout at the park on the Bay side of Dock #3, where all the old "townie" retirees cook the venison burgers for the next generations, and the popular three-legged race and the gunny sack races are held. The greasy pole event was remembered, but no longer observed, where a $20 bill grand prize awaited atop a 50 foot greased telephone pole – an event I won as a young girl.

The beer-fest at the Fire Station just to the north of downtown and adjacent to the old courthouse where our high school friends now volunteer to make this a safer community still goes on with fire truck rides for the children and grandchildren - something that most small town people do in America on the 4th of July. The things that my sister had always enjoyed with her sisters and her friends, and later her children and her husband, until this year when Cancer came to stay and forced all of us to be patient with our lives beyond what we could imagine possible and remember what we had to give each other.

She never acknowledged that week that she was missing anything, that she was being unfairly cheated out of anything either. She just patiently waited for us to take turns returning to the old homestead, where we were camping out for a week, to tell her about the activities and be with her as she existed in her "stupor" world, sleeping away hours in her "makeshift" bed with a window slightly ajar for those cool breezes off Lake Michigan. She asked for very little, demanded even less and so we all tried to do more. She mostly slept and on occasion joined us at the old weathered picnic table out back for a small bite to eat, sometimes the "pasties" made famous in this small part of the world. There was always a spot open and someone special missing when she could not make it to the table. Her spot was quietly acknowledged as we began to accept the situation more easily. Still today, that is the case.

We were able to stay in our old family home at the Point the rest of that week since it did not have tenants moving in for a couple weeks. This home is still owned by one sister, even though none of the sisters have lived there for decades. Thank God, this home is still in the family and there for us when so much was taken away.

We "camped out" in the old homestead on State Street with sleeping bags and camping cots, a card table and a few lawn chairs. We loved it just the same, even though the old place had an eerie feeling of being only vaguely familiar. Too many tenants had occupied it since Mom moved out – our patience was being tested again.

The small house was still adorned with the covered back porch facing the woods, walled to protect from snow drifts because that entry was the one used in the winter and kept clean for visitors. The front porch and door that were hardly ever used on the Lake side of the old homestead seemed stuck in time, and the large picture window on the Lake side showed us again that magnificent view of the five mile long expansion of the Mackinac Bridge across the Straits-of-Mackinac - a true natural wonder we so easily took for granted until life became so special and fragile.

The old and large black wrought iron kettle hanging in the front yard at the corner of the house, where Dad had carefully placed it many years ago, badly needed the touch of summer flowers. Mom would have planted pansies. The rock garden at the corner of the long driveway, that had always had the first sign of spring with brightly colored tulips popping up between the snow patches, no longer resembled life in the 60's. That innocent time for all of us when we thought the hardest thing to deal with in life was getting to stay out past curfew. Instead we were dealt the hand of patiently watching God call one of us home to His house knowing it was not for us to ask why.

The clothes lines in the backyard drooped almost to the ground with green paint peeling off the old bench and that red box of wooden clothespins looking back at you with signs of long ago. Mom was always telling us we needed to get the clothes in before it rained. The red dollhouse and big wooden swings Dad had made for us as little girls resembled life in the 50's, when our yard was where all the fun was because we had all the "stuff", not the sometimes solemn place it was today when all the patience in the world did not make life acceptable.

The red dollhouse, with its pitched roof and French windows, had been there for 40 plus years with all its miniature features just for little girls, and big girls. It was slowly sinking into the ground and taking in wild grass through the wood floors - a true replica of what had been and what was slipping away. The swings that Dad made also included a tire swing dangling from a large braided rope, certainly the hit of the neighborhood. The small sandbox area was no longer flanked with two-by-fours like it used to be, the sand was dirty and the big spruce trees heaved to the ground. Small town Americana with its clocks stopped and a time warp that we do not want to let go of was getting away from us. We did not have the answer as to how to stop this disaster and certainly not the patience to let it happen.

Never cut what you can untie.

Joseph Joubert

The inside of the old homestead had an uncanny feeling of being abnormal. There was no permanent furniture, and carpet and paint that was "not ours" since it had been a rental property for many years and tenant improvements abounded. Tensions were high at various points, a family in distress trying to live together decades later when great loss was lurking. I found my patience being tested, especially with people coming in and out of the door to visit someone, sometimes to visit her in her makeshift sickbed and not realizing just what it meant to be so sick. They tried to talk about the right things, say the right things and make her laugh, but this was more than a time for waning patience, it was down right stressful for her to say the least.

I still wanted this summer to be the way it was when Mom made the best potato salad in Mackinac County, from "scratch" of course, singing songs while she cooked like "The Chattanooga Choo Choo" song. Dad would be home on occasion for a visit from working on the Lakes, he was a tugboat captain, part of a dying breed at the time. He loved to take all of us to the Moose Lodge for fish fry on Friday night or prime rib at The Flame restaurant to show off his family in his proudest moments the way it used to be and the way it should be, the way I looked for it to be when I came home oh so many summers to escape a week of Arizona heat. No amount of patience would bring back what was or could have been, but patience would make it somewhat tolerable for today as life played out the way it was meant to be and, thank you God, we were patient enough to wait for those signs of what we were to do next.

We did do the preverbal cookout in the back yard, shucking corn on the back porch and grilling chicken on the old rock fireplace Dad had made many years ago when the house was built in the '50's by Dad and Grandpa. It was a tall fireplace style in large rock from Lake Michigan, a structure like none other that has stood through 50 years of harsh winters in the North Country. We bought beer and Vernor's ginger ale to enjoy at the old weathered picnic table, to cool off in temps that were only slightly warm and wished we had Mom's famous potato salad instead of the "store bought" coleslaw we found at Glen's, but we had my brother-in-law's smoked white fish dip to round off the menu. This is what would now be the good times we could remember and cherish since she was still with us ever so slightly.

Another day we did the infamous trip to Mr. C's for a "Big C" burger, fries and a shake, piling into one car for the short trip up the highway, knowing it was so hard for her. She was quiet and in her own thoughts much of the time, not the way any of us will remember her or choose to honor her, we will see only that toothy smile, twinkling eyes and hearty laugh.

A poignant moment appeared that day when we were all sitting around the old picnic table after we returned with our burgers. She commented how she would like us all to live together again in the old house, that we too could do that just like others in town were doing - those that had not left or had come home again to be closer to family. The lump in my throat was too great to tell her there were many times since I had left home some 30 years ago that I wanted it that way too. That no matter what had transpired when we were growing up and how many times I wanted to leave home, home was still where my heart was too. Just like her, it surely was where I had wanted to be many times after I had left home as a young woman. With all its warts, it was still a warm and safe place.

She had always made it a place to return to by living there down the Beach from the home where we grew up, the house that was just as welcoming to any of us. This time we had to welcome ourselves home and take care of her any way we could with love and kindness, devotion and understanding. We had to muster up all the patience God had given us.

For reasons I still do not understand, I was not able to return six weeks later for the funeral. I knew my sister would understand why, even if no one else did because she knew me and understood me. She loved me and I loved her.

We were the same and yet so different, but we had always been patient with each other.

She had been more than a sister to me many times. She had been a soul mate and a friend, a confidant and an advisor as well. Just as important, I had to be patient with myself and believe that a few years later I would write this therapeutic book and release myself from any pangs of guilt. It was partially finances and what I perceived as obligations that kept me from coming back only six weeks since my vacation trip, but mostly it was a lot of just plain fear - fear that this was really happening, fear that it was the end, and fear that I would feel so alone with her gone. I was not seeing the big picture, which I usually did, and I was not thinking clearly, as I did most of the time.

Was that Chemo fog and stupor contagious?

I regretted that decision, and that regret complicated my closure of her passing. But I knew that God had a plan for all of us. God helped me to never forget those important words – God's plan. God's plan for me now is to share her story, to be her voice, to leave her legacy and to give to those who are walking this same journey, either in her footsteps or in mine.

After being crippled by my fear to make that decision, I was prepared for all the ways I would be approached by family about finding a way to return because it was "my duty." I would never forgive myself – again the Catholic guilt - because it almost makes it worse to have to say "no" ten times than it does to accept the reality of the situation and why you cannot do what is expected of you. In the end, life goes on and we all deal with our guilt, grieving and anger in our own way.

Does that decision allow for closure of her passing possible or even necessary? I have tried desperately to be patient with the progression, to take the anger and the denial and the questions and the longing in stride. The continuous longing for answers is part of the first phase of loss and part of the grieving process. Getting angry when you learn one more person has Cancer helps the need to not forget and helps in someway to keep the "race for the cure" alive in your heart and soul. Denial she was really gone saved me from going crazy, but there came a time when I knew it to be true - like during the holidays or her birthday in January when I no longer looked for the funniest birthday card or the nicest gift I could afford for her. I knew too I would never again receive one of those homemade treasures she made so lovingly and gave so freely to me and to others on many special occasions.

How can it be over when I think of her everyday? I truly believe that nothing related to a human's life is ever really over; it is always evolving in our hearts and minds, fitting into our lives differently, but fitting just the same. Thinking of her everyday is a healthy way for me to live my life for both of us, to keep her spirit alive, to leave her legacy and to let her walk along with me on my journey. This book is my way of saying thank you for the memories and my way of saying she is alive in me and always will be.

Why would I want closure anyway? Life does not go on without her, life goes on because of her and her gifts to all of us, and to the sisterhood in our family. I don't want closure, I just want peace of mind that she did not die in vain and will not be forgotten. This book will leave a legacy and memory of her and a chance for all of us to grow as people, as "sisters" for her; it is for my sisters, my female cousins, my girlfriends and their women friends. This book is for all the women I have met in my personal and professional life that have touched my life. Men friends are always welcome into the "sisterhood" too.

I did not anticipate that I would deal such a long time with no form of closure having not attended her funeral. I had only expressions from others as to what really happened that weekend at home the end of August when she was going to the light. I had only their perspective as to what it all means when you watch death unfold. I had only their take on what transpired as she passed over. Hearing the stories of a room full of family, some immediate, some not, watching the process as she began to pass gave me a feeling like no other, an empty and lonely feeling, farther down the well than ever before.

Would she have wanted more privacy? Would she have preferred the choice that was made for her?

I was told her young sons were present too, watching from afar as she lay solemn in her stupor in the bed made for her in the Dining Room where she had been for a long time. The Lake and the Bridge and all of the area's beauty spread out for her embrace from the picture window as she made her way to the light. I am sure it was surreal; so removed from what was her vision of the Point only a few short years earlier. I envisioned myself lying next to her on that makeshift bed in her Dining Room, talking to her in a whisper, patiently saying good-bye in my own way. I saw myself getting smaller and smaller as if I was wilting away with her.

I attended noon Catholic Mass that day at Arizona State University, the small and quaint chapel on campus, a busy place that day as it was the first week of school. I had no other place to go; I was 2000 miles away. It was very warm walking across the campus, at noon the last week of August in Arizona. This was a place she had visited with me many years earlier to roller-skate the afternoon away on a spring vacation when the campus was almost empty, unlike today.

I was alarmingly unemotional as I sat in the small pew, seeing the priest in slow motion. I am sure I was numb and fearful because this was the end, but this was not to be the time when the full impact of her loss would be felt. This was only one small day in August when I would try to figure some of this out in my mind and heart and soul.

> *Patience is the greatest of all shock absorbers.*
> *The only thing you can get in a hurry is trouble.*
>
> *Thomas R. Dewar*

I am blessed with the realization and knowledge that my sister and I knew each other well enough that I can today be comfortable with my decision and patient enough with the rest of the closure to take it as it comes. Part of my closure is my "Sister Scrap Book." I have been "scrap booking" for her and for me since her death, everything from old family photos, her obituary, favorite poems and the cards I received at the time of her death.

I also have a "Sister Box" with all the things she gave me that I want to cherish and keep forever such as the white, bubble style bicycle helmet with the lavender race visor she loaned me to do the MS150 bike ride when she was in remission. I did the ride in her honor and found peace and patience I did not know I had in me. Finishing the race was inevitable because she was riding with me those two days at 90 miles on Saturday and 60 miles on Sunday. Her white helmet had Mom written inside of it with a felt marker; it was so much like her. I felt safe on that ride because I was so grateful for my health and my life, and for the chance to share it with her while she was still alive and had her faculties about her. The distance paled in comparison to the journey she had taken in her battle with Cancer.

The "Sister Box" also includes her Barbie, Ken, Skipper and Scooter dolls, their suitcases and their clothes, those she purchased and those she made as a young girl. They are safe and warm with my own dolls. The white and purple floral design afghan is in that box, as well as a pink needlepoint of strawberries in a can, both items that were displayed in my condo for many years, but are always mine to enjoy. There are a couple of stuffed animals that I took from her room after she passed to the light, again joining some of my own stuffed animals forever. Rounding out this collection is a circular sign with a frog in tennis togs holding a tennis racket that says "gone to the courts," something fun she sent me a long time ago, and an old and now stale balsam pillow from a trip we took to the Traverse Bay Woolen Mills store to shop one more time like we did most of our lives.

Although the "Sister Box" is in the store room, it is in no way put away from me. It is just down the hall from my condo door and easily assessable when I need to be near her. Through these tangible items I can find the intangibles, the love and kindness, patience and generosity she gave so freely, feeling them close to my heart.

Finally, I have some of her American Indian jewelry, a turquoise and silver ring, and a couple of silver bracelets bought in curio shops in Michigan, just different enough from the American Indian silver jewelry I have from Arizona to make them special forever. They are items I proudly wear regularly and feel close to her and home when doing so.

And then there are the broaches, those costume-type blue colored stones she wore on blazers and hats. Although

I rarely wear them, they are in my jewelry drawer; I see them often and smile at their sparkle because they represent her flair for the eccentric which was so critical to her charm.

I returned the next summer hoping to say goodbye to her at her Garden burial near the Lake, adjacent to the side yard of her home. The way I envisioned it many times did not exist; my patience was tested again. Her husband was not ready to let her go and create the garden, or the fountain and the memorial that was being planned for her final resting place. Her ashes were still in the urn on the fireplace mantle, next to a framed quote from the Book of Proverbs that I had sent her during her illness and an exceptional picture of her at a happier time that encompassed all that she was about for us – free, charming, funny and playful.

The memorial Garden was in the early stages of design and development, the plan for the fountain was there, but just the base was sunken in the ground and in place. The Garden had no sign of flowers or tending, just the shrubs brought by nature that were part of this secluded spot she had always loved. But it was her special place just the same. It was just over a little old wooden bridge that had been there for a long time. The trees and shrubs were a bit overgrown giving me a feeling of privacy for meditation, and a chance for all of us to get used to the idea that this is where she will be forever and ever.

The donations for flowers that would later be planted had surpassed all expectations. They would wait for their time of planting, remaining at the Flower Shop just down the road. It was known in town that donations were to go for the flowers if not for the Cancer Society or the Library. Her neighbor and good friend was to be the curator of the Garden since she had such a beautiful home garden just next door, and had been a friend and neighbor for most of their lives. We would all take our cue from her.

The old bridge and the overrun of weeds made the soon-to-be Garden feel as though it was hiding, waiting to awaken when the ashes arrived with her Spirit. I knew I was being tested and I needed to step back, check my patience and realize that the finalization of the Garden resting place would not happen in my time line, but when it was supposed to be, when my sister was ready to go to the Garden and when her husband was ready to let her go. Patience is a virtue. I knew that too well. I also knew that I may not be present for the burial of the ashes, maybe no one but her husband and children would be present. Privacy was now being guarded and respected more than ever in our family.

I had so hoped to come back for a memorial that first summer after she passed with the ashes ready to rest, the Garden completed just as I thought was planned, with the fountain flowing fresh streams of water everyday, and the flowers in bloom in all possible bright colors. But that was not God's plan. Because I did not physically attend the memorial I had a tremendous need for some form of "burial" remembrance, of closing this chapter, but that scenario was not to be played out for me until I took her Spirit to Ireland a few years later. My patience had met the ultimate examination.

Thank God, the little old bridge was still standing and the Great Lake Michigan again lapped up on the rocky shore, while the distant sounds of the Ferries and Freighters made their way to the Island and along the horizon. The pungent smells of the Shoreline were ever present, even though the waters had receded over the years due to drought. The sight of the water line out farther than previous summers engulfed the sound of Sea Gulls crying, and made my heart ache. Even God's country had to change.

There is no patience equal to the patience of God.

Oswald Chambers

My summer vacation the year after her passing was stressful. Her boys were difficult due to their own justified frustrations, and life seemed in an uproar at the old homestead. There were not a lot of hugs and few times to talk to her boys, their choice, and so my patience was again tested. They were struggling with their grief and guilt, and nothing I could do gave them any comfort. I had to be patient with them and let them be where they were at that moment in their lives. They had every right to grieve in their own way, in a place only a son could find after losing his mother at a young age, a place I did not know nor would ever find.

It was a sad time for our family; we all missed her desperately and played out life in many ways that did not seem to be the "right way" for any of us. We tried to find a typical summer experience in the Upper Peninsula with a trip to Mackinac Island to smell the famous fudge cooking, and to see a time gone by still being played out with a long walk up to the Grand Hotel. We tried cooking out in the backyard like we had done so many times before along with a trip to the Sand Dunes for a swim, but it did not help; it was rushed because we were all trying too hard to make it the way it was when life was so much easier. We were not patient enough with grief and what it wants and takes from you. We all knew it would never be the same without her wit, charm and laughter, and we did not like it. We resented the fact that we had even been asked to be patient for a moment with Cancer living amongst us.

We knew we needed to carry on for her by participating in the 24 hour "Relay for the Cure" event for the Cancer Society held on the old track field at LaSalle High School on Portage Road. We were joined by aunts and uncles, and friends and family. We did the relay as best we could to make an effort to complete the 24 hour event. Things were strange to say the least with her name and photo on Luminaries in several places around the track. Just walking along the track required patience. As we walked along the track, we read over and over again names of those who had passed or were suffering, and thank God, those too who had survived. I also knew I should have been present the year before when it was her turn to give the talk to the faithful about how Cancer had taken so much, but yet made her whole, and how she had found God and her Faith in all of this and how this Cancer was changing her life and the lives of every one of our family members. I should have been there to support her, but who knew it would not come this way again.

I was still busy in my world 2,000 miles away, calling and supporting her by phone and planning to visit the next month when it was more convenient to my schedule. I needed to be patient with myself and understand we make decisions that are right at the time and we must live with them. God is patient with us always, who are we to not be patient with ourselves? God help us to be patient with all these memories for they have their place to teach us what we failed to learn up to that point.

Patricia L. Brooks

She gave me the gift of patience.

Patience wears out stones.

Gaelic Proverb

Take time in the space provided to reflect on your patience of others and situations in your life at this time.

Patience! The windmill never strays in search of the wind.

Andy J. Aklivis

CHAPTER NINE
The Gift of Courage

It is a lovely thing to live with courage and die, leaving an everlasting flame.

Alexander the Great

The last time I saw my sister alive was supposed to be at the least a comforting week of summer vacation for me "at home", a chance to regroup with her and family, and to settle into what was really happening to her and to all of us. It was to be different from the way it had been for so long and yet we knew it could only be God's plan. As hard as it was to accept God's plan, I knew that it was the ultimate test of faith in this type of situation. We had to do this for her and for each other; a family that had tried desperately to keep faith alive had to show courage in even the most difficult time.

She was getting ready to go in for more chemotherapy, that poison, that destructive drug, that torture, that inhumane treatment that is so antiquated and yet deemed still necessary and the only answer. All the signs of her body longing for that poison, which is the "trap" of Chemo, and her mind saying - "no more, I want to be here with you and know what you are experiencing" - came rushing home as I first saw her so humble and small. This Chemo, this poison, this imprisonment was something I silently disagreed with but knew that it was not my place to say "enough already." I was the oldest of Dad's girls, but I was still floundering as if I were a child in all of this. As much as I wanted to do the right thing, I also wanted to do the selfish thing and take control which is not courageous, or is it?

Was it my place to step to the front?

What rights do we have as sisters?

What chances do we have to say she is part of me and I am part of her, this is wrong, inhumane and we need to stop this now?

How could more poison, more torture, more inhumanity to man be the answer to anything?

I flew into the little airport in Pelston via Detroit in the same small prop commuter airplane I had taken so many times with its spats and sputters and a humming sound like no other, almost a comfort to what was ahead. But this time it was different. This time my senses were so strong, a sure sign this entire vacation would be viewed in my mind forever, an old movie that would just keep playing.

The large spruce, pine and balsam tree tops were their deepest shamrock green, the color I look for when I come home after living over half my life in the desert in Arizona. The Great Lakes were crystal clear with their sparkling topaz blue color, a Michigan summer sky blue so brilliant for a moment you could forget that life had a haze on it and that a lot of the brightness of a beautiful life was fading quickly. The propeller plane's familiar sound was as loud and constant as an old outboard motorboat on the big Lake over a still night in June, a constant whirl of energy driving me closer to what was not going to be even remotely what I had enjoyed so many times since leaving there 30 years ago. The courage to go home had come quite easily to me because it really was the best part; she had the hardest part of all, saying good-bye to all of us.

My senses seemed to be more sensitive than ever at this moment, surely God's way of making me more ready to gather up the courage I was going to need for what I prayed was not the last time, but knew differently in my heart. Although family and friends often saw me as courageous, I knew this was going to be the real endurance test of my wits and strengths, as well as a time to show my weaknesses, those vulnerabilities when we want to be little girls again and life will not let that happen.

Her husband met me at the Pelston airport, alone that early evening, without her and without the boys. Because of daylight savings time, the sun was not quite setting and the stillness of that night at dusk was noticeable and eerie to me. This greeting style was a first, she had always been there to meet me when I came home and walked down the steps of that small prop plane. The waiting room was filled with people, some familiar faces and some thinking they knew me too.

His daunting look said it all, "prepare yourself." His only comment was "she is waiting for you at home." Waiting for me at home was such a scary idea; she had said so many times on the phone that she would be at the airport. How hard it must have been for her to know she had to wait there because she could not make this seemingly short trip and let him go on the 30-mile drive without her - the littlest things that mean so much can be taken away so quickly.

We took the familiar route home down that same two-lane wooded road, through all the little towns that brought back fond memories of life there in the 60's when we were young and healthy and looking forward to the wonders of life. We traveled quickly along the Lake side of the state towards the Mackinac Bridge, seeing its vastness from many miles out, a site that always gets me anxious to be home, and across the Bridge to the Point, that section of the Upper Peninsula that juts out under the Bridge on the Lake Huron side and yet tries to still be hidden from the summer traffic escaping the southern cities of Michigan.

We were trying to have happy small talk, catch up on the trivial goings on of my hometown, bringing me up-to-date on the latest small town gossip which allowed me to escape anything I had left behind that I thought was so important in the whole scheme of things just hours before boarding my flight. I was trying desperately to look forward to seeing her in that Chemo-fog-stupor condition I so despised, that baldness, that paleness, that quiet and longing that was not she, that pathetic state that was cheating her out of the life she deserved. I made every attempt to have the courage to ask all the appropriate questions about her health and condition and state-of-mind, hoping the answers to these unwanted questions to be more than my expectations, but I knew that was impossible. These were ugly questions that would solicit ugly answers. With or without courage, we had turned the corner on this evil disease and we knew it had won.

Courage: The lonely virtue – the rib of Himself,
that God sent down to His children.

James M. Barrie

I entered the house at the Point from the back door pantry room only to see her sitting silently with a desperately longing look on her face, fixed toward the Lake. God bless her – she was bald again, pale as she had been at any other time or even worse, and much, much thinner with her frail hands fidgeting in front of her. Please God make her stop – she is acting like an old woman – she is not this person I see. She must be more courageous. She has had so much courage for all of us.

Why do I have to watch her play this role?

She was sitting so still on the edge of that old worn and cozy couch that was so reflective of the lifestyle she loved, comfortable, not too organized, but planned. The couch was as it had always been, strewn with an afghan she had so lovingly made with a matching pillow, and her Cocker Spaniel Patty McGee nestled at her side. Except for the obvious condition of her body, I felt some comfort in something familiar.

The dining room with that magnificent picture perfect view of Lake Michigan and the Mackinac Bridge out the front window was now converted to a sleep area and "sick bed" for her - an area where she was almost on display for her courage, and revered as well for what she was gift-giving to us. It was a spot that took some getting used to for a private person like me that had lived alone for the past 25 years. I was feeling almost violated at the thought that "for the grace of God go I," this could have been me as easily as her. Lung Cancer does not always pick the obvious woman, although she had been a reformed smoker for 12 years, this type of Cancer takes many women for unexplained reasons. Lung Cancer takes more women than men with no explanation and it does not forgive past discretions.

Her favorite brass bed had been taken down from the loft there at the "cabin" and placed by the picture window for her comfort – if that was possible. An antique end stand I am sure she found in a farm auction in southern Michigan or a thrift store in Petoskey was strategically placed - "junk hunting" was one of her most enjoyed pastimes. This "symbol" of one of her small pleasures was covered with a white linen cloth and many pill bottles – surely more bottles than any one person should have to tend. There were other items strewn about as well, such as a book on inspiration, "get well" wishes in a multitude of cards and carefully written notes, and a small red clock which seemed so out of place because it did not know that time had stopped for her and for all of us.

This was to be her last place of rest so she could look out through the large picture window, west down Lake Michigan to the Bridge, that priceless view that we all love but took for granted when we were growing up. She had the courage to give the memory back to us and allow herself to be placed there where we could once again appreciate even the smallest of joys – such as watching the white cap waves lap up on the rocky shore and the cars cross the Bridge on a sparkling summer day.

She beckoned a faint smile when I entered the room and encouraged me to hug her, no strength to hug back with her arms but I could sense a hug from deep within her soul. This was a repeat performance; we had been here before.

God, why did we have to cross this way again?

God, what purpose does remission serve?

She had already suffered so much. I suppose remission is just a chance to catch your breath before the struggle starts over again. I knew at that moment I needed to have the courage to accept the things I could not change and be there for her unconditionally.

Just how much poison does it take to teach us that poison is not the answer? When was it going to be my place to step in and say no more? What obligation or responsibility did I have to her as her big sister? What right did I have to verbalize anything about her treatment? Was she waiting for me, her big sister and close friend, to step in or had she resolved herself to courageously accept God's plan?

This has haunted me for a long time, enough to search deep for the answers. The answer came in God's own timeline, not in mine. I believe today she was not waiting for me to step in because she had the courage to face Cancer when it raised its ugly head again, only nine months into remission, and the faith it took to be courageous. She was willing to do whatever it took to the end, never wavering with doubt. I chose to believe this or I would have been tormented by the thought that I had failed her dearly, that I had not taken enough time to think of her and pray for her.

I did not believe then, and still do not believe, that after remission from lung Cancer when more Cancer comes to you that more Chemo and radiation are the answer or would make much of a difference. As much as I did not want to accept the inevitable, I also did not want there to be no quality of life for her in the end. This time should be for reflection, for prayer and for laughter. This time should be to embrace her in mind and soul if not in body. How I wished for her some time to think and reflect and write, but that was not to be, that was for me later and not her then. It was my responsibility to step in later and write this book, to give the gifts of sisterhood to all who ask, to be her voice, to leave her legacy and keep her memory alive. She gave me the ultimate gift, the courage to do just that, and good or bad, here it is for all to see. She did do this anyway, in her own way because she knew me and knew I had to tell her story. She never said keep quiet – she knew this day would come.

How do I know that there is not a secret diary or notes to her sons or her husband to be found sometime down the road? Surely I was not the only aspiring writer in the family when we were growing up. I always believed she had untapped talents, like so many of us, just waiting for the chance to emerge if only we have enough time and courage to take that chance. For her, it was not meant to be except through me.

How do we know her inner most feelings aren't recorded for any of us to have when we have the courage to hear them? She always seemed to wear her feelings on her sleeve, but she may have just needed the courage to keep some for herself and some for us too.

How do I know there is not a manuscript hidden in that old house, her story in her own words? She was notorious for having kept the old and forgotten, and valued what they were at a time gone by and how they could be of value to us now. She was courageous in her efforts to keep the "simple" life alive for all of us.

Who am I to say, or any of her sisters or friends to say, we deserve documentation of her thoughts? With all that she gave us, she had every right before Cancer and after Cancer came to her to have her special place with only space for God. She did not even have to say good-bye; we knew she hated to go.

She was not a private person in our eyes, but maybe, just maybe, we have much more to learn about our little sister. This too will be revealed in God's time and maybe because she often loved to read and write notes, she is already recorded in more than our hearts and minds. She could also be writing through me. I do not take full credit for any of this writing and pray I have the courage to be so humble with any good that comes my way from this book and share it in ways that would make my sister smile.

*It takes as much courage to have tried and failed
as it does to have tried and succeeded.*

Anne Morrow Lindbergh

**Why do we try to put back into working order
something we think is broken and make it the way we
believe is the way it should be?**

Cancer is a personal thing and comes each time in a
personal way to those it takes. This much I do know. This
much I prayed to accept. It is not for us to ask why. God's
plan is not always revealed to us when we think we need it,
but when we are ready and deserving of it. Bad things do
not happen to bad people or to good people, they happen
to any of us, despite our lifestyles or because of them. To
continue to say she quit smoking 12 years ago and this
should not have been a factor is unfair to her, to her legacy
and to all the courageous moments of her struggle.

She knew God's plan from the beginning of her bout
with Cancer and she chose to fight, maybe more for those of
us having a hard time with Cancer coming into our family
than for her to hold on to physical life. She had the courage
to believe a spiritual life is so much more enduring and if we
are lucky, we will accept that gift of courage from her. She
had a positive outlook on life and so much of that sustained
her many times, but she also had her moments when it took
everything she had to be courageous and she gave it her
everything.

Her courageous actions were everywhere, in her day-to-
day activities with pill taking and vomiting and pain patches,
procedures and surgeries, and in the way she handled
friends and family - with love and compassion, kindness

and honesty. The gift of courage was to prove itself worthy of being one of the greatest gifts she passed on to us.

Good friends are good for your health.

Dr. Irwin Sarason

She allowed all of us to live out our lives with her Cancer as we preferred, especially her children who played out their role in all of this just as they chose to by spending time with their friends, attending school and learning life's lessons as teenagers. She kept up the smile most of the time, she kept a positive outlook most of the time, but when she needed their touch or a kind word she had the courage to say I am a human being going through Hell and I need you.

Despite efforts by all of us, her children had to cope with this situation in their own way. They had to find their own courage from their mother's example, yet be teenage boys in a crisis. All I could do was try to be a loving example, the way she wanted it. To be available to them with no expectations, the way she knew it had to be. To say I love you as easily as saying hello, the way she would have done it every time had she just had the chance to be a regular mom. The job she was born to do so well.

I have had to address my anger head-on regarding her doctor's decisions and what I saw as misjudged decisions. These decisions I perceived in the beginning brought on the anger for all us. It is so easy to blame the General Practitioner when he or she is not the Specialist, to blame the Hospital in a small town when it is not a big city (ER) and to blame those around her when they are in denial or just trying to hack it like everyone else. Anger is that human emotion with a negative connotation that is so necessary in our lives to be truly human. Thank God I had the courage, from her, to be angry when I needed it to survive. Anger set me free to move to acceptance and the courage to move on through the maze of Cancer.

Why did the local doctors miss this evil? Was it just more than they could deal with at the time? I am sure; and it is too prevalent in small town America, so they keep hoping that one more from the small community has not been bitten and needing their limited help.

How could they miss this terrible disease and call it pneumonia? Cancer is so prevalent in our society; one in four is the frightening statistic. We are all touched in some way, and we want it to be someone else. The doctors are no different; they are people with families who live with Cancer. They dig deep for courage just like you and me, yet it takes the whole journey of Cancer in your life or your family to come to this realization. Nobody said it was going to be easy and it surely isn't.

Why did it take nine months and four doctors to determine what was really happening to this young and vibrant woman? She had eluded major health problems her entire life, delivering healthy fat baby boys in record labor time. My conscious mind told me speaking out would cause detriment to too many, yet for so many of those early days I spent hours on the computer researching Lung Cancer and getting more and more angry with the statistics and stories. Finally, with the help of God, I had the courage to stop doing that and to accept things as they came to her. This was one of those times in all our lives when we had to move on and accept fate, to embrace destiny and do the best we could with what we had at the moment, to say our prayers, be positive in our own way, to trust in God and have the courage as she did to live within these limits. We all had to find the courage it took to stop saying, "you need to be more positive" and let people be who they are and where they are with a situation such as Cancer raging.

> *Better to remain silent and be thought a fool*
> *than to speak out and remove all doubt.*
>
> *Abraham Lincoln*

She was the youngest sister, the one who was not supposed to be the first to go. Her boys were barely teenagers. She had not met their girlfriends, their future wives or the grandchildren that will come someday. She would not attend their high school or college graduations, their weddings, the housewarming parties for their first homes and so many other wonderful milestones in life.

Why did they use that old line "You are too stressed with your life that is why you have lower back pain?" All the research I found on the Internet on those lonely nights when she was first ill clearly stated a sign of Cancer in your body is lower back pain, just like bruises, cuts that don't heal and persistent coughing. It is worth noting here that only 10% of women over 40 ever survive even five years from Lung Cancer. She was climbing Mt. Everest in a pair of "flip flops," and we all knew it.

How could treating any pain with an antidepressant be the answer? Pain is God's way of saying something foreign has come in to His "temple," your body; we must find a way to remove it, deal with it or let it go, not deny its existence and "band-aide" it together for awhile, and not bother to question it endlessly. We must be courageous at all costs.

The anger eventually subsided somewhat; but I was still feeling my sister was an experiment, a guinea pig as she took her journey down the Cancer maze. I was trying to come to grips at the very end. I had accepted the fact that a more quality life could not be, and she knew it too. Quality of life and Cancer is an oxymoron. No matter what you do, say, feel, believe, or imagine – it is what it is, the pits!

What was she thinking all those months when she was alone with her Cancer and her thoughts and reflections, even when people were physically and emotionally around her? Probably that she was living outside a life, watching a tragedy on the stage of life – one where the script would not be edited for a happy ending. She knew this was more than a melodramatic part she was to play.

How was she grappling with the thought that she would leave us behind? With grace, I tell you, pure grace! God bless her for all her courage under fire.

Would her sisters try to fill her place and maybe fail miserably or do a good job? She loved us and family; she knew we would do our best.

She never complained to us; she never showed us her anger about Cancer and she never made any of us feel like we could do more. Of course, the anger was there somewhere. She had to go through the stages of denial, anger and sadness before acceptance, just as we did - and even more so. I do not recollect her asking for anything except what we had to give her at the time, those parts of ourselves we were willing to let go of so freely and offer up to her. She allowed all of us to choose our courage, how we would participate and how we would give of ourselves. She experienced her faith to the end and was a badge of courage for all of us. Our little sister needed us, but we needed her too and we all knew it. This was a turning point in all of our lives.

Love in the heart wasn't put there to stay;
love isn't love 'til you give it away.

Oscar Hamerstein II

During her remission she made a conscious decision to become more than a practicing Catholic and attended the necessary classes to be a full-fledged Friday "fish eater." This was a courageous decision to make as an adult, being a "come back Catholic" is not easy for anyone and certainly not easy for someone who is trying desperately to understand God's plan when it is not the plan you had seen for yourself. It is a true test of your faith.

She had attended the Catholic Church most of her life, and like others attending the church had not been baptized. Our parents had another sister and me baptized in the church when we were babies. We had Godparents to prove it, but no proof as to why she was not included in this rite of passage for Catholics. Our parents were like so many in early marriages with three young children, some things just did not get done. There were no baby pictures taken at a studio of her either, yet as the first born there was one of me.

Why did they not baptize her, the baby and Dad's namesake? I believe it was God's plan to have her baptism at a time when she could fully understand the impact of what that meant to her faith. The two of us who were baptized have Godparents who have always been in our lives, and are still alive today. Baptism is considered a top priority in the Catholic Church as it is in many other faiths, but somehow lost its importance when she came along because life was probably hard for them then as it was most of the time.

They must have been at a difficult place in their lives or in their relationship to have not done this; baptism is that important first step to a life of faith in the church. She also came along five years later than the "middle sister", and a lot can change in life in five years for any couple.

Dad was Catholic, but not devout, and Mom was Methodist and devout. They had agreed to raise the three of us that were his children Catholic, but to have us attend public school. It was commendable and courageous of my sister to make the effort to become a Catholic during her time of serious illness and to be a beacon of light for the others in her "come back Catholic" class. She was preparing in her own way to take that last step in life, to "cross-over" as my grandmother used to say. It was as if she always knew there would be a time for her to take up the cup.

Do we just cross the line where the light starts and hover above when we cross over, watching life take place?

Keeping an eye on the rest of us, I deem, is so much of what she does now. I believe that she has not missed a thing and is nearby daily in our lives and enjoying every minute of that time. She is there to see the good times and the bad, and the ups and the downs that we as a family will experience no matter who is present. I sense her presence often, cherish those moments and am grateful I have the courage to tell you I know she is here.

When others are happy, be happy with them.

The Book of Romans

She kept her sense of humor when the rest of us were losing ours, and she mustered up a smile more times than I ever thought possible. The courage to smile is taken for granted by all of us at different times. A smile does not take a lot of effort; it is less muscle than a frown. She seemed to smile pretty easily, even in those last days, and thank you, God, her sons have inherited that wide, toothy smile, that electric bright lights on smile that is inviting and comfortable. She also knew that a smile makes people wonder what you are thinking and she liked the mischievous part of a smile, that "keep'em" guessing attitude that brought fun to us many times.

Joyfulness keeps the heart and face young, a good laugh makes us better friends with ourselves and everybody around us.

Orison Swett Marden

I remember the time, during her last few weeks with us, when I was changing her catheter bag in the bathroom. I was somewhat uncomfortable in doing it, but knelt on the floor next to the toilet bowl looking up at her. How awkward this was for me, something I could never have imagined doing. She had her panties and shorts down around her knees, waiting for me to help her, as I never knew I could. She peered down at me with those big hazel eyes and that wide toothy smile. Her comment was "and we thought we knew each other," her way of saying all her inhibitions had been taken away, or maybe she had let them go anyway. We both started laughing. I suppose that is reflective of the blessing of growing up with all sisters, those intimate things happen and seem so natural. But more importantly, we had crossed to a place in our lives where we would never turn back. Our lives had been changed forever as we realized her body was slowly leaving the place it had always been and was now dependent on apparatus too odd to even be counted.

We were literally camping out in our old family home at the Point that week, near Lake Michigan, since it was in between tenants and vacant for a few weeks. That night we had been making plans to go down to the Beach to that special place at the Straits of Mackinac, just a block down the hill, to watch the July 4th fireworks across to the south side of the Bridge in Mackinac City and again at the lighthouse end of Mackinac Island. One more desperate attempt to make life like it used to be when we were little girls and everything pretty much happened as our parents promised it would be most of the time. Knowing and not knowing that a little more of the fun times could be the last of the fun times for us as sisters was a heartfelt blow.

*A little nonsense now and then
is cherished by the wisest men.*

Willy Wonka

Her life culminated into a love fest when the Old Catholic Church on Church Street, across from her former home overflowed the day of her memorial. Everyone in town wanted to pay their respects and say good-bye to one of their own. It was an event, just as it should have been. They needed to recognize her courage.

The love also showed itself when many well wishers signed their names on the back of the new shingles for the house called by her namesake. They would be a part of her place called home for a long time. It was at this get together after the funeral, a party time as she would have wanted it to be, a chance to reminisce, laugh and share stories that many had the courage to tell stories on her. Stories from the heart of the Irish were being told over and over again, and a part of life that she loved very much was being lived for her.

Most importantly, she had the courage to have a wonderful second marriage and raised her boys with fierce abandon. She loved being a mom, taking part in their school activities and sharing in their joy and sorrow. She loved having a home that was warm and inviting, a home that said a family lives here, come on in for a moment. Those stories were told too.

She loved being in our hometown community of 3,500 people where everyone knows your name, and where she could give back and be a part of something such as organizing the neighborhood block party each year. Her neighbors will long remember her contributions.

Her success was celebrated in the response by the community to her courageous battle with Cancer and the way they came together to embrace her compassion. They were relentless and vigilant in being of service to her and her family by bringing dinner to her back door and leaving it on the sun porch - easy to do since no door ever needed to be locked. Those donated dishes came and went sometimes with a name on the bowl and sometimes not for they always found their way back to where they had come. These warm dishes were just as necessary as any other medicine she could possibly need. Compassion is a strength to be shared, and the courage to share it is the real blessing.

She gave me the gift of courage.

They say they climb mountains because they are there. I wonder if it would astound them to know that the very same reason is why the rest of us go around them.

S. Omar Barker

Take time in the space provided to reflect on your courage and a time when you have been courageous or have witnessed courage first hand.

Courage is the first of human qualities because it is the quality that guarantees all others.

Winston Churchill

CHAPTER TEN
The Gift of Gratitude

*So much has been given to me; I have no time to ponder over
that which has been denied.*

Helen Keller

The last time I saw my sister I attempted to say enough,
to say the right thing, and do even more to show her how
much I cared. I am forever grateful for even having had the
opportunity.

Could I have done more for her? This is a question
that still haunts me, a question that is part of my feeling of
loss. There is no answer to this question.

Did I hold back from doing the exception? She did
the exceptional things considering this was new territory, a
rough road for all of us, she did them for us. In the whole
scheme of things, what really matters is being grateful for
the chance to have some time to say good-bye. It could have
been much worse; she could have been snuffed out of our
lives in an instance. She could have been taken away from
us even more tragically.

Why does this despair happen? The self-doubt, the
longing for answers and the wanting to feel secure in our
decisions is surely part of it. Maybe it is God's way of forcing
us to evaluate who we are and how we should grow, so those
who have gone before us still live in us in some way.

Why do we wrestle with what someone else will think?
The need to get approval, to be accepted seems natural. The
need to be assured we did our best and all that we could have

done is human nature; it is who we are as people to have needs like these.

Why do we torment ourselves because we may not have done it perfectly? We did it our way not the way the next person would have done it. Their way could surely not be better. Be grateful, my friend, that you even tried. There is no right way, there is just life.

Who decides who is right? I choose to believe God guides us in these situations and forgives immediately if we fall short of some mysterious standard. I am also grateful for the opportunity to be in touch with the most precious of feelings when I recall my sister and my life with her and without her.

My sister's life makes being grateful easier because she freely shared with me how she felt about her Cancer and what she lived with each day of her disease, the light-headedness, the feeling of not being connected to the world she once knew, the fog, the nausea, the hair loss, the weight loss, the deadened taste buds, the physical weakness, the pills and shots, the pricks and pokes, the port in the chest for more "poison," the dependency on others for sometimes everything, and the subdued pain, but pain you knew was still there. She was grateful for every day she experienced this Hell on earth because it was still better than the alternative at that moment.

She told me she had gotten used to Cancer as things went along, because those patches on her back were a constant reminder the "body temple" had been invaded by an alien - an alien that could not be squelched of course, unless it was meant to be, unless it was God's plan. She told me she was grateful for the wonderful life she had with her family, raising her boys and knowing the "good life" that some never experience. She told me she lived for today.

These revelations were not for sympathy, but to give me an opportunity to appreciate what it was to have my health, to be forever grateful for my energy, to thank God for my life just the way it was, and to live my life for her and for myself then and always. I am grateful for every breath I take, for every day I jump out of bed with a place to go and things to do, for every time I enjoy a special meal with a friend or a great movie with a meaningful message that feels like it is just for me. And I am also grateful for every opportunity I have to do even the most mundane things such as weekly errands, watering my plants, combing my hair or reading my mail; these things that were taken away from her long before her last breath was taken. These are mine for the asking and I am truly grateful.

Write on your heart that every day is the best day of the year.

Ralph Waldo Emerson

In my gratitude I look forward to my next 50 years, God willing with wonder and delight, knowing that a lot will happen, most of it will be good, magnificent and purely wonderful, and that she will miss so much. I commit in my heart to her to be there for her sons' graduations, weddings, childbirths, promotions and life changes; to be grateful for my 50th birthday, which occurred six months after her demise because she would have given anything to change places with me and hit the big 50; to see the years ahead as gifts and treasures and be grateful for whatever that will bring while every moment saying thanks; to always smile and count my blessings; and to be loving and friendly.

That summer of her passing I was still praying she would come to visit me again in Arizona, that there would be one more chance, one more time since she so desperately wanted to visit again too. She knew she was going away forever and that the things we sometimes take for granted, such as visiting family another time, would not come back to her, except in spirit. She was trying to muster up the gratitude she had for what we had experienced, but I know it was terribly hard. She was a real trooper in her death, as she was in her life, but it was not easy.

She knew that life was short and getting shorter by the minute. She knew we should never put off precious things in life that touch the heart and make life worth living, such as writing and reading, listening to music and appreciating the arts, in exchange for those things in life that can be taken away immediately such as work, career, and material things of all kinds. She had truly been grateful for what some might have called the simple life. She never coveted another's position and was always grateful for what God had given her materially, spiritually and personally. She was to be commended for recognizing the value of the simple life, another lesson I have learned from her and for that I am also grateful. She lived that life to the fullest.

I did not accept her failing health condition at that time either, even when I was faced with taking her to the hospital emergency room twice in three days and hearing the nurse say the "H" word - Hospice, which is a sign of the end. The "H" word did not register for me or I would not let it register its true meaning. It was too soon. I was not ready to let her go. My sister did not acknowledge it either because she knew I was not ready. She was so silent in those days, a distant look in her eyes and a longing that could not be filled. She was already outside of herself and it was frightening. Despite all the gratitude I was trying to muster, I knew I was not grateful for much of this scenario.

I remember sitting next to that sterile hospital bed as they put the intravenous (IV) tube of Saline solution into her now thin and very white arm. In an attempt to comfort her I was stroking the top of her hands while hoping to make me feel connected to her in some little way. Her pale and calm hands were longer and thinner than I had ever remembered. Her nails were still incredibly healthy, almost translucent and angelic. They looked a lot like Mom's hands used to look, dainty and graceful with some of the veins at the top of the skin, which is supposed to represent active hands. Ironically, her hands had been still for a long time, or maybe not, maybe they had been actively praying and the raised veins were there to prove it. There was still life here. That was something to be grateful for this dismal day.

I recall sitting near the end of the sterile bed as they put in the catheter with the ease of a seasoned surgeon. A catheter was for old people, for really sick people; they must be mistaken putting a catheter in my sister. I was trying not to react to what seemed so bizarre to me. Two nurses were talking and working away as if it was a project for the church bizarre. Some of their conversation that morning was surely out of place for such a major event. Did they not know this was my little sister here, fighting for her life? This was something that happened to the terminally ill, not to someone so young, someone in our family, someone who had such a great spirit. Denial is a wonderful thing; it allows us to ease into reality when reality is just too painful. It gives us the chance to get there in our own time. Denial is a good thing. I am grateful for denial and recommend it to anyone moving through the maze of Cancer, if even for a little while.

Gratitude is something of which
none of us can give too much.

A. J. Cronin

At one point during my last visit with her, when I was sitting and watching her sleep from the end of her bed, she sat upright and asked, "What is going to happen to me?" In a moment of clarity, I carefully answered that none of us know God's plan, that we sometimes had to let life happen and maybe that was what we were doing here now.

Why could I not say more? Why was I not able to dig deeper into my faith with a better answer? I know how grateful I was for that special moment to attempt to be better than my best, to have a chance to rise to the occasion and be everything she had hoped I could be, the big sister with all the answers.

Why could I not tell her she would be around forever in our hearts and thoughts? We would see her again sometime. She would always be loved and missed and remembered in everything we did and enjoyed. We were grateful for the years we had with her with childhood memories that were only ours. She would always be watching us; we knew that too. There was no right or wrong answer, just a moment in time that will be forever etched in my brain.

How many times have we wished we had said something else or done something else when opportunity presented itself? I am so grateful God forgives our "human self." Sometimes, an opportunity to give of ourselves happens too quickly. We are only human and need to be able to forgive ourselves when we miss that opportunity, be humble enough to do that because God has already forgiven us. We just need to do the best we can do.

The look on her round and pale, still freckled face, and the tears in her eyes that no longer sparkled will always be vivid for me, that gaunt and soulful look, one which was sometimes a wounded puppy look and one that sometimes mustered up peace. There were times, in those last days, I would watch her sleep and twitch, mouth moving and eyes fluttering, wondering what it was that she was dreaming and where it was that she was "living" at that moment. She was preparing to pass on and greet the ones she had loved that were on the other side; you could sense it and see it in her face. I choose to believe that to be so, that we do see the white light and hear the welcoming call to God's table.

She was never angry outwardly about her difficult situation, but inwardly many times you could feel her frustration when she was waiting for us to return home where she was confined to her bed or a small lonely chair or when she was being force fed too many pills. She never made any of us feel like we were not doing enough, or too much, whatever that could possibly be. She was always grateful for any part we had in her final experiences.

She knew we would do more or less if we just knew what that was for her. She was grateful for our presence and had always made family a priority. She knew caring for the sick and dying was new for us, although she had done it several times with our parents and her husband's aunts, never thinking the tables would turn so early in her life. She had empathy for our thoughts, as she had walked those steps too, and we are all grateful for that gift!

How happy a person is depends on the depth of his gratitude.

John Miller

I have finally come to grips with those moments of frustration and that is why my spiritual contact, my connection with her is so grand and so important. I think of her everyday. Something always reminds me of her. It might be an afternoon shopping in a consignment shop; she loved to shop and find a bargain. She relished the idea that she could beat the system and find the ultimate bargain. She was proud of this attribute long before it became fashionable to be frugal because being fashionable and trendy was not something she did or appreciated; she valued being true to herself. I am truly grateful for that gift as it has freed me of the traps of commercialism in many ways.

The reminder of her might also come with a warm and sunny day at a craft fair perfect for browsing and appreciating others' talents. She had her own giant talent for making crafts and gifts that we all loved and cherished, many I have had for a long, long time: the purple and white flowered, crocheted afghan; the pink and red needlepoint of strawberries in a basket framed in bright pink; the hand-sewn peach silk and vintage lace teddy lingerie; and the maroon and navy blue quilted carrying accessories that were unique and useful for traveling.

Christmas gifts from her were always unique because you knew she had started making them back in the summer months, and that much thought and love had gone into the making. She had real talent in creative ways that added softness to her that we all appreciated. I was grateful for her efforts, maybe envious that she tapped into her creativity so early in life. It is only now, several years after her passing that I have been given the freedom to explore my own creativity to great heights. God gives us things in His time and it is not for us to ask why or why not but to pursue those things fully as I have writing this memoir for her.

The reminder of her can come when I am out to lunch with my girlfriends; she cherished her girlfriends and enjoyed meeting mine. The girlfriends she made in high school were her friends for life. Unlike me moving around to four states in my life, she came home to our small town Americana, in the Upper Peninsula of Michigan, that place so many people think belongs to Canada, God's country saved for those of us who know its magic. My gratitude extends to her here too as there is always a place called home we can come to because she's there.

She chose to stay within the confines of her youth and yet allowed those personal relationships to grow and blossom. She knew the importance of sustaining relationships with women, sisters, friends and neighbors. This was life to her, this was living. The conversation, laughter, tears, storytelling and plenty of joke-telling was evidenced by the response to her and her illness, both before and after her passing. The outpouring of love and kindness still goes on with mysterious gifts of kindness appearing at the back door when least expected. She has not been forgotten in that small community. There are many who know gratitude because of having known her and her efforts to give back to the community.

He who forgets the language of gratitude can never be on speaking terms with happiness.

C. Neil Strait

Long after she passed, there was credit available at the floral shop just down the road from her "burial garden." The donation account for the burial garden on the Lake which will supply flowers for a long time is being used again and again. It is my guess that will never end.

I have no doubt she is happy for my good fortune since her passing. I sense it when I think of her. She always wanted more for me and never begrudged any good fortune that came my way. On the contrary, she usually hit me between the eyes with a jolt of reality if she thought I was not doing the best thing for myself. She tried desperately to get me to be more grateful for the little things in life. She succeeded and life is good. What freedom when gratitude for her life in mine came to my heart!

We can pick our friends but not our relatives, but in this case I could not have done a better job myself in picking a sister. I had someone in her who understood me better than I did myself. It is true, we see ourselves easier in someone else we trust and love because their perspective can be a true mirror image of ourselves.

How could I possibly think she did not know me, maybe better than I knew myself? She had matured into a responsible woman from a wild and crazy gal, and I am grateful to have been able to see that happen to me too and to experience it in my own life. That transformation was something we could share - that opportunity for character building, that metamorphosis to self-actualization, that is so rare and yet so valuable and necessary in all of us.

Why do we sometimes take our closest confidant and friend for granted? Get angry at them? Probably because they let us be us. I know this type of support and friendship is not always so in siblings. I never felt the rivalry or competitiveness that I have seen with my friends and their siblings, for that I will always be grateful to her. She was a dear friend and never had a problem with that part of our relationship; she did not criticize my wrong decisions and there have been a few. She understood me more than anyone else in the family and that I miss the most and am most grateful; having been able to talk to her and be myself whenever being me was the best therapy. A trust that is hard to duplicate. This is the real story of my sister - her willingness to make choices for the better, all the time watching out for others. This is what I am most grateful.

The holy passion of friendship is of so sweet and steady and loyal and enduring a nature that it will last through a whole lifetime, if not asked to lend money.

Mark Twain

She would love the man I am with for life and she would appreciate his humor, wit and ideas as much as I do. She would be grateful, as I am grateful, that God brought him to me. She knew him like I know him. We were looking for him for me, praying he would just knock on the door and stay a long, long time. He did just that when I wasn't looking. My relationship with him would make her happy – it would make her smile.

She always wanted me to find someone older, more secure emotionally and more attentive and engaging. She wanted me to be fulfilled, as she was in her second marriage to the father of her boys. She appreciated her good fortune, was grateful for everyday and did not take it for granted. She knew in her heart that she deserved that good fortune, but she could be grateful and humble just the same. Thank you God for giving me the courage to tell her she deserved happiness.

She had known the challenges of relationships in all forms. She knew she had reached a junction in the road when she made the decision to stay in Michigan and raise her first son, a decision I am sure she made without any second thoughts. She was eternally grateful for motherhood. She also knew she did not take the easy way, but the best way and she traveled that road and never looked back, enjoying everything along that incredible journey. The miraculous birth of children, the beauty of a precious children growing up, the many challenges of them maturing and the realization that they are their own people; she loved being a mom and took her parenting role seriously, and was grateful for the opportunity to be a great mom.

I remember her telling me once that sometimes she would pinch herself because things were so good, so exciting, and so enjoyable. She had had her rough spots just as I had and as many of us have on a regular basis. I assured her many times that she deserved the good things that had come her way - a loving husband, two wonderful children, a home and life she wanted and enjoyed, and a life in small town America, where we grew up in modest means, in a place she could truly call home. She was welcomed home when she came back to the Straits of Mackinac for the rest of her life. She was a good person who had done some wild and crazy things in her youth, just as many of us do. That was only a small part of who she was and those who loved her knew that to be true; she did not have to keep proving herself to any of us. We were grateful for her spirit and all the times it showed itself to us.

She gave me the gift of gratitude.

The next time you're feeling down, think about all the terrible things that didn't happen to you.

Barbara Johnson

Take time in the space provided to write a grateful list and to reflect on all the things you have to be grateful for at this point in your life.

Love one another.

The First Book of John

CHAPTER ELEVEN
The Gift of Acceptance

Forbearance should be cultivated tell your heart yields a fine crop of it.
Pray for a short memory as to all unkindness.

Charles Spurgeon

She took chemotherapy and radiation again after remission when Cancer found a new area of attack, the front of the brain. She somehow accepted what was happening and persevered. She experimented with herbal remedies and concoctions from loving friends and family as well as far too many pills - large pills that would have choked a horse.

She faced hair loss and baldness again with a vengeance. She sometimes even relished in the uniqueness of her head without hair, wearing special hats and headgear on some occasions, but many times just staying in the moment and accepting the baldness and all it represented. She was never too vain to be who she was wherever she was at the time. We all grew to admire that about her, maybe even envying her and wondering if we could ever do the same should God call upon us to be tested.

Had she set the benchmark too high for some of us? Had she made it almost seem easy or acceptable to fight this battle? I know she was not foolish enough to lose sight of reality, and probably always knew her days were numbered. During her Cancer years she was a changed person. We knew she could never be the same and we could not either, and for that alone we will always value her for that gift of acceptance.

117

We held each other so tightly that cool summer's morning I had to leave for Phoenix; I felt frozen in time. Lake Michigan glistened from the bright morning sun and despite the summer's beauty, it was cold and gray in our hearts.

> *If you haven't any charity in your heart,*
> *you have the worst kind of heart trouble.*
>
> ## *Bob Hope*

Her boys, their friends and her husband were already in the vehicle and ready to go. We had so little time to say good-bye for eternity. She knew it and I knew it. She looked so frail sitting high in the front seat of the Explorer. It was almost as if she did not exist as a real person, but someone in limbo waiting for an answer that would not come. The boys were going to a rock concert in the city where she would receive her "poison" one more time. They seemed so much more interested in sleeping, or talking about the concert they would attend that night or the shopping they would do at the big mall before the concert than the fact that this moment would change my life and their mother's life forever.

Was this their way of handling the worst of things? Of course, it was their choice. What could have possibly prepared them for this anyway, this bizarre state of affairs? These are young teenage boys trying to have some sense of normalcy in a truly abnormal world. They are merely teenage boys losing their mother to this appalling disease – a disease that compares to babies found in dumpsters and kittens duct-taped to the curb. There is nothing valuable about Cancer for anyone trying to cope, except the value we can place on what we learn about ourselves and where we are with acceptance of life and God's plan for us. This disease is so repulsive that avoidance is the only option so many times until we can reach the shore of acceptance and come on the land of life hoping for some feeling of safety.

She would again patiently wait for them, while they had their fun that night. As always, she was the devoted and loving mother even when her energy was almost nonexistent. This would be tiring, but maybe her last chance to do a mom thing with her precious children and she could not miss it. She would go along with where they wanted to go and do what they wanted to do. She was still selfless in this life when no one would expect even a kind word from her. She had accepted those responsibilities completly and to the end.

She would take her "poison" and then spend hours waiting for them outside the concert hall with her husband, finally continuing with the two-hour drive home late that night when she would be entering the Chemo fog and thoughts so far away. How I ached for her, for this to be her day, relaxing on the Beach with a good book or stretched out on the old diving Raft floating in front of her home - the Raft that had not even been launched that summer, but "beached" on the rocks instead - also looking misplaced. She deserved so much more. How had she come to accept God's plan?

How hard it was to step away from her grasp though weak and failing – just like a fire ready to go out at any moment, it was weak. How hard it was to say good-bye, knowing it was the last good-bye - the finale, the end, with no encore. There had been nothing made more clearly to me than that moment, a realization that it was the end, infinity, eternity. When we can see the light at the end of the tunnel, and it is a beacon in the night like the old Lighthouse across Lake Huron at the tip of the Island, we know we are home. She knew God was calling her to the light and she was accepting his hand. I was not only losing a sister, I was losing a friend, a dear friend, a confidant, a soul mate for sure and a part of me that no one could replace. I also knew that keeping her in our hearts is the greatest and most important thing we can do. Some things you just know and feel, embrace and accept.

> *All friends are not for life, but if you have a true friend, you have a life.*
>
> *Lois Wyse*

Nothing about that situation was reality, or the reality that I so desperately wanted for her. It seemed as if I were experiencing a bad dream, and if I did accept what was happening at that moment, I would wake up and it would be unbearable and true.

They had a long drive that day I said my fateful farewell, a long drive to the hospital in Traverse City - 90 miles on a two lane road in Northern Michigan is not fast travel, but it is oh so beautiful. The green of the North Country, the little towns and homes untouched by the change of time bursting with flowerpots and antique wells must have made it somewhat comforting for her – she loved that area. Living in a small town complicates treatment for any disease. It adds to the time and energy needed to accomplish each step in the journey with Cancer; the travel time is part of the journey. It makes each appointment a lengthy one, but maybe that is meant to somehow prolong a life that is slipping away. The specialists do not find a place in a small town, the sick need to seek them out and go to them. Accepting what appeared to be poor service for my sister from the medical profession was also a great challenge. Most likely it was all part of the acceptance I needed to swallow for myself.

Patience often gets the credit that belongs to fatigue.

Franklin P. Jones

Nothing was easy in this situation, but she was doing what needed to be done to accommodate the doctors and her treatment. Why did she feel she had to accommodate anyone? I suppose because she had accepted her fate and chose to play the role God had given her in this life – at times knowing it was futile, but always holding on to her faith. When they said one more time, she had more "poison"; when they said more Radiation, she had more burn and when they said more meds, she choked down more pills made for a horse. She had accepted her fate, God's plan and lived out her life teaching us lessons of acceptance with every step of this painful journey. We were to learn about ourselves as much as anyone - the lessons of acceptance and tolerance for a situation that cannot be explained.

Her last doctor was an "older hippie-type lady" as my sister would say. She portrayed a Bohemian person of sorts. She had an artsy, folksy manner - reminding my sister of Mama Cass as she still chose to dress in circa 1965. Mama "doc" had an office to match her personality - including a dog nearby and "knick-knack" things of animal life that made living through anything bearable in my sister's eyes. Man's best friend had served again as the comforter of the sick and dying. In all her pain, my sister found some solice in this environment of times gone by.

She did not look well enough to me to make the 90-mile trip, let alone have that "poison" one more time. She was so thin, so pasty and colorless with a whisper of a voice from a once demonstrative, vibrant and outspoken person. What was the point of this anyway? She gave me a slight hug from a once strong and sure body, and a faint smile from a once beaming personality. "Where have all the flowers gone, long time passing?"

She whispered timidly in my ear repeatedly as I clung to her next to the vehicle's door, asking me to come with her on this leg of her journey, and to not get on the airplane. If I left then it would finalize so many things. I will always remember that faint whisper and see that look of longing in her now distant eyes for things to be different. Different in any way as long as there could be just a little more time – just a little more time to be sisters.

So many times I have wished I had done just that, said "no" to returning to Arizona at that very moment, said "no" to my commitments and responsibilities for another week or another month and said "stand still" to those "man-made" things I thought were so important, and thrown passion and faith to the wind and broken out of what I thought I needed to do. But I did not, and so I live with that decision and all the sadness I carry with it. Sometimes there is nothing more that we can do and we accept life and let it take its course adding only our love and friendship when that is what is needed most.

A friend loves at all times.

The Book of Proverbs

Why is it that we keep these responsibilities? It is because that is what we are taught to do if we are to be dutiful and respected and that is what we practice in life because it is the American way. The "different drummer" part comes later when real life comes into perspective, when we get our priorities straight and realize what is most valuable to a full and balanced life.

Why at a moment in time such as this, do career and household demands seem so trivial in the whole scheme of things yet they draw us back? It is because we know subconsciously that life goes on despite these hurdles, and these obstacles. She would have wanted it to be that way - once more making the best of things, taking the bull by the horns, and pulling up the rear. There are so many more of those trite sayings that come flooding back to us when we are searching so longingly for the right thoughts and prayers. She would want us to go on as well because she knew we would always take her spirit with us in our hearts..

Why do we try to maintain some semblance of order when Cancer takes all the order out of life and gives you only chaos? It is because we really do not know what to do until we can accept the situation just as it is and go on with our lives when we can see the balance of nature, the good and bad, the paradox of joy and sorrow and know that there is more of the "good stuff" than the bad.

I knew in my heart and mind and soul it was the end, but like so many of us when we share the dying person's last weeks I too needed to hang on to that last ray of hope, to not quit until the miracle happened, even when I was having a hard time accepting the inevitable, to accepting fate and destiny or whatever you chose to call God's plan for our lives.

Life is hurrying past us and running away,
too strong to stop, too sweet to lose.

Willa Cather

This prayer has helped me many times: "God grant me the Serenity to accept the things I cannot change. The Courage to change the things I can and the Wisdom to know the difference." On other occasions during her final days, nothing worked and so I just felt the pain.

I learned this prayer many years ago and my sister learned it later, but we both knew it was appropriate now and that asking - "why?" - was futile. There is no - "why" - when it comes to God's plan, but there is a plan; there is a point when accepting God's plan is best for everyone and everything.

She gave me the gift of acceptance.

Joy is not in things; it is in us.

Wagner

Take time in the space provided to reflect on just how accepting you are of your life and the challenges it presents.

If you tell the truth, you do not have to remember anything.

Mark Twain

CHAPTER TWELVE
The Gift of Faith

Faith is not trying to believe something
regardless of the evidence: faith is daring to
do something regardless of the consequences.

Sherwood Eddy

About a month after my sister passed, as usual I woke early at home alone. I woke slowly to what appeared to be a beautiful and angelic-like vision. I did not open my eyes or even move for what seemed like an eternity. I felt her warm presence in the room as if she had been there all along. I felt her strength and spirit - that same feeling we get when we know someone is watching us intently, examining with love in their hearts or admiration or approval in their thoughts. You know what I mean, those kind looks that can make your day and even better make you feel good. I knew she was always watching because she understood me so well and always had an honest and straightforward answer for me. She knew me so well and I knew her as well too.

This brief moment in time was her way of saying I am still here, and not leaving any time soon. She wanted me to know that nothing was past, and that nothing is lost around the corner in life, and that life and death are one; they are connected and the process for all of us. Fearing either takes away from both. Both need and will be experienced. She said she wasn't going anywhere and she wasn't kidding! She was there as surely as you are where you are reading these words.

I did not need to open my eyes to see if I was dreaming; I knew this was not a dream or a chance meeting but an encounter, a cherished familiarity that I would always honor. I knew it truly was happening because the gift of faith had been given to me by my sister. I was very comfortable with that gift, that souvenir of her life in mine. I did not pray or talk or move. I just let myself relax knowing I was not alone in that room. I stayed in the moment and did not acknowledge what day it was, what time it was or what kind of day it was going to be. I gave myself the freedom to be fully absorbed in the experience.

It was that same feeling I remembered from childhood when the robust fire's Dad made glowed in the old potbelly-burning stove in the garage, or warm chocolate chip cookies Mom made so perfectly were served with steamy cocoa. It was that same feeling I remembered of snow covered mittens that dried on wooden hooks near the big furnace in the utility room while the snow lay as a crystal white billowy blanket just outside the rear window of the old house. It is that same feeling we get when we share a robust laugh and a fond childhood memory with a sibling and know we are home!

She was not pale, or thin, or that heartbreaking, non-communicative shell she was her last days on earth, she appeared to be at that moment angelic, content and of the faithful. She was not impartial or only existing, as she was so often those last months due to the drugs she was told to take daily. She was her old self, whimsical, smiling and challenging, with a clean freckled face and short dark brown hair shining atop a strong stature. She was the way I choose to always remember her. She was the way she will be committed to my memory because that is the choice we have in this life – take them with us as we wish. She would like that idea because she loved people who were accepting of everyone regardless of opinions or beliefs, especially when it came to faith. Her presence is felt by me everyday just like the sun and the wind. I remind myself of her often and always have our special visit to sustain me.

Just around the corner, yes, and in the same room, absolutely. I talk to her regularly in my heart and in my mind - she loved a good conversation. I know that I am not the only one who does this because it is a natural occurrence for those left behind after the death of a family member or a friend. What a gift of faith it is to live as we please knowing it is okay with God and most of the rest of the world to talk to the deceased, to be mature enough, and self-assured enough, with yourself to not give a 'flying leap' what somebody else thinks when you know in your heart it is the right thing to think or do.

Why is it when we talk to God, we're said to be praying, but when God talks to us, we're schizophrenic?

Lily Tomlin

God works in mysterious ways: nothing is a coincidence. Nothing happens in God's world by mistake. There is a plan for all us: there is destiny and fate - that is what my gift of faith has taught me. Sometimes to really accept these truths there has to be a leap of faith such as:

- Accepting why a healthy, happy and vibrant woman in her early forties must succumb to Cancer, leaving behind a loving family and friends.

- Permitting fate to come to pass, and accepting that it has nothing to do with you and everything to do with you.

- Acknowledging God has a plan for all of us and that this was His plan for her.

- Seeking what it is that I am to learn from this experience and having the faith that the answer will reveal itself in God's time not mine.

- Understanding how my faith will be tested in the future.

- Believing I do not have to ask why and get an answer to be sure of my faith.

These truths I have contemplated for some time - taking time for quiet thought. This small part of life is a blessing - a gift from God.

My first revelation that she had come to accept these truths came during her remission when she chose to take the "come back Catholic" classes at the local church and go through the entire understanding your faith program just as a child would have done. She was comfortable being baptized in the church as an adult. Cancer had taken the few inhibitions away that still existed, and she was a sponge for faith. She knew she needed to recognize her faith in this world to leave it here for all of us. She was proud of this effort, but never arrogant or boastful.

Any seemingly disparaging comments by her about the church were always made in jest, covered with a lot of love and humor. She had Catholic jokes in her repertoire, but used them tactfully and sparingly. She practiced her faith and lived it to the end, both in the church of man and the church of God. She understood the difference and made no excuses for either.

I choose to believe she knew from the very beginning that she was terminally ill and that her passing was inevitable.

God's time was two and a half years, the doctor's time, six months. She had work to do in that short amount of time and gifts to leave all of us. She had the courage to say "don't give me six months to live," and the faith to know she could prolong it with her belief in God and all things good. She had bits and pieces to do for all of us while putting up her fight, and for that we will be forever grateful.

She gave me the gift of faith.

Faith does not wonder why.
God has not done anything that needs to be explained.

Pamela Rosewell

Patricia L. Brooks

    Take time in the space provided here to reflect on your faith and how others have impacted your life within their faith.

Faith is the bird that feels the light and sings to greet the dawn while it is still dark.

James S. Hewitt

CHAPTER THIRTEEN
The Gift of Happiness

Happiness often sneaks in through a door you didn't know you left open.

John Barymore

Two more years had passed very quickly since her passing and I returned "home" to Michigan for her oldest son's high school graduation and a long anticipated family reunion. It was the first time I would be back in the old high school gym since I graduated some 30 plus years earlier. So many memories rushed to me as we made our way there that spring.

The LaSalle High School would now seem so small and stopped in time, yet so much the way I remembered it, even though several additions had been made to it over the years. So many reminiscences of a happier time gone by for me ran through my head and so many thoughts of whether my nephews shared happy memories of high school there too. Anticipation and excitement came flowing in to me as we entered the building that beautiful warm evening. How had these years of her illness impacted her boys' most critical years, those high school years? We could never know and only pray that God picked them up and carried them and that happiness had not eluded them during all of that time. She should have been there too – this moment she so deserved.

It was haunting to me to think that some of my sister's happiest times were here in this old building and during that period of her life. Did her sons value and appreciate their high school years as much, or would that come later? Did they even have the chance to build happy memories while grieving? Probably not, since their lives had become consumed with grief and pain - whether they acknowledged this or not - it was a Hell on earth. There is no control, just a hiding place in our subconscious mind, when time alone is all that is available to us. We must choose our happiness; we must look for it and welcome it, and we must accept nothing less no matter what the situation. Thank God I have lived long enough to realize this wisdom and to know God's grace works in mysterious ways.

The graduation ceremony was about accomplishment, dreams, and plans for the future, just as it was in school commencements all over the country in late spring that year - just as it was when I graduated and when my sister took her diploma on that small stage decades earlier. It was to be a time of happiness and joy, a time of excitement and wonder.

Had her sons begun planning their futures or given much thought and consideration during these hard times to what they would do now that three years had passed away since their mother's death? One would be going on to college in the fall and the other the same route in two years. They have so much potential, and for many years of their young lives, have done great things with artistic and creative talents.

How I ached at the thought that Cancer and death had changed so much for them; maybe even stolen happiness and their unique creativity for a while. This moment in time was actually robbing them of the innocence of high school and teenage years. Stealing what little naiveté is left at that age when the harsh reality of life hits you in the face. When there is no explanation for the sadness, for the ache, and the longing for it to be different is excruciatingly painful.

One can only hope and pray that they accepted her gift of happiness – the gift their mother freely offered to the end. One can only hope and pray that the gift of happiness offered to all of us will be shared with them because it is a God-given right to be happy in this life.

It is still quite cool and crisp the first of June in the Upper Peninsula of Michigan, not quite warm enough to swim in Lake Michigan, but beautifully in bloom with spring's flowers. The forget-me-nots and the dandelions along the shoreline, and the geraniums on many a sun porch are bursting in color and eager to welcome you home. It is so refreshing to see and enjoy these beauties with the thought of summer just around the corner. My dad always said the Upper Peninsula had two seasons, winter and the Fourth of July, but I like to remember four seasons because spring is my favorite. The Lake sparkles like a kaleidoscope at that time, and the town begins to emerge with summertime buzz. Storekeepers are putting our new signs and awnings begin to emerge and sway in the breeze. There are spring showers to contend with or maybe they are more to enjoy, a chance to feel that quiet patter while those light showers make things clean and glistening.

Everyone seems happier, excited about another tourist season that will add exhilaration to the town and revenue to sustain another winter. The little motels and restaurants are freshly painted and adorned with colorful windsocks, flower pots and "the old red, white and blue" - to give that feeling of new and yet the familiar as we arrive with anticipation of another wonderful week at home.

This trip was also a time of family reunion for all of us, a time my sister should have shared with us in more than spirit, but that was not meant to be. We would all be home that spring for a few days together - the way it was in the Christmas of '97 when we came together 13 strong to support her when Cancer first arrived and took her hair, but not her spirit, took her strength, but not her hope. She was obviously absent at this reunion – absent from the photos, the plans, the ceremony and the party, or was she?

There was happiness at this reunion – she must have been there. We could feel her presence and sense her spirit. We could see her "toothy" wide inviting smile, the smile we missed so much. That grin we longed to see one more time, that happiness we cherished, the endless jokes and wit and humor that brought happiness so many times to our family. She may have been silenced but she was not gone and certainly not forgotten.

Cheerfulness is the habit of looking at the good side of things.

W. B. Ullanthorne

She was going to miss a lot of memorable experiences with the boys growing up without her - there was no changing that reality. What we had to do was change our attitude about how we would deal with this life altering experience and choose happiness. It is what she would have chosen for us. Happiness is what she would have insisted upon if she could have had any part of the last five years of family decisions.

Happiness is part of the last phase; the acceptance phase that we had almost conquered was the hardest. We were all going to miss terribly that part of our lives that had been taken away. I knew I had to think happiness when I thought of her because she would have needed it that way for her boys. She was happiness. She was the final stage and she would remain with us.

We were all committed to bring happiness to her boys at every opportunity – that was expected and understood. To do it for her was my pleasure. To laugh with her old friends in her boy's presence and show them joy was a blessing. This weekend was no exception and would make that possible.

We are blessed if we can make another laugh. She did that so well so we all tried to keep the laughter going by reminiscing about the past and having fun in the moments we had together, then and now. It will be two more years before we assemble again for her younger boy's high school graduation. A chance to do it again, and maybe do it a little better because we will be healed just a little bit more. It will be a chance to be a family in the best possible way.

I brought my dear friend with me on this trip, the friend she would have loved and laughed with and the one she knew in her heart before I knew him. The one I have allowed to bring true happiness to my life. The one she always said I should be looking for or not looking for because he would appear. She believed that strongly because of the course of events that had shaped her life. I knew she was right, thank God, and I had been willing to wait and then let him in when he came knocking. She prayed too for my happiness.

He had heard a lot about my sister from me before we left for that trip, and he was anxious to meet her boys and my family. He looked forward to visiting my hometown and experiencing its long history, over 300 years, and to sharing the abundant beauty with me. He understood my pain, he had known loss too, and appreciated my faith that things would be improving and that happiness and joy are everywhere if we just let them into our hearts. We fulfilled our plans to not only attend the graduation, see family and some of my old high school friends, but to enjoy the celebration of her boys' transition.

We visited historic and wondrous places such as St. Anne's Church on Mackinac Island, the Father Marquette Museum in downtown and Fort Mackinac also on the Island. My sister cherished these spots so much I had to see them again in a whole new light. She was a great cheerleader for Michigan and spent most of her life there in the North Country with all its beauty and wonder. Snow, rain or sun, she found ways to enjoy her life and bring happiness to every moment. She loved snow skiing with her boys at Nub's Nob, snowshoeing alone on the beach next to a frozen Great Lake to meditate, bicycling on Pte. La Barbe Road with the majestic Bridge as a guide and sailing with her husband under the Bridge or over to the Island, but especially circling the area where Dad's ashes and my Cousin Bobby's ashes had been thrown many years before.

In her memory, that week we also went to Taquamenon Falls, along scenic Lake Michigan via US #2, taking in the copper colored water that runs strong at the Upper Falls. Copper because this is copper country, although no longer mined it is still a part of the history.

Then on to one of her favorite spots in the Upper Peninsula, Whitefish Point on Lake Superior and the Shipwreck Museum where the Edmond Fitzgerald story lives and reigns. The Fitz sank many years ago during a 100 mile an hour storm in the Gales of November. The ship has not been raised, but the bell was brought up to the surface to be duplicated and made as a tribute to the men who died. The original bell is being placed again in the water. She loved to tell this story.

Putting my toes in the coldest water I could imagine that day was my way of being her, if only for a minute – my way of sharing a little happiness with the others on the beach who did not dare to do such a thing. She would have liked it just the same.

The Ferryboat trip to the Island on another day brought back a flood of memories about her. She was always game for a trip to the Island. There are no cars allowed on the Island to disrupt its quaintness and smell of horse manure and fudge, and all its history dating back over 300 years. A beautiful walk to St. Anne's Church and Mission Point along the boardwalk and harbor off Lake Huron gave us a moment of silence and a quiet time down memory lane. These small pleasures gave her great happiness, and I wanted to grab some of that for myself, feel her presence one more time and live that gift of happiness she so freely gave anyone.

Main Street on the Island is just the way it was in the 60's, with a chance to purchase the infamous Mackinac Island fudge and Island sweatshirt - just as we had done so many times before as young girls. And of course, we had lunch at the old Iroquois Hotel in the historical dining room, with window seats facing the harbor full of sailboats that have traveled from as far as Chicago or Detroit. With all the brightness of a summer day coming through the windows and leaving the cold chill outside, we experienced the romance of a long time ago. Little bits of trivia that brought happiness to my sister will remain in my heart forever.

We had a wonderful time, just the way it was, not perfect as it never was, just good enough for the memories that will last a lifetime and a chance for me to feel her presence in those places she appreciated visiting each summer. That step back in time we all need on occasion to feel alive again – especially on a vacation that is for so many reasons a time to regroup, relax, slow down and go back home.

Talk happiness. The world is sad enough without your woes.

Ella Wheeler Wilcox

The natural garden and rock wall fountain for her resting site were now in place by the Lakes Huron and Michigan at the Point near the rugged Beach that she loved so much. The wooded backdrop to the beach area was the same as it had always been, large spruce and pine trees hiding the small garden from the flow of traffic in and out of the house. The grass and shrubs were just overgrown enough to give a feeling of "The Secret Garden" mystery – one of her favorite books. A large pot of magnificent flowers stood atop the spot where her ashes had been buried in their urn, but surely not forgotten. Her spirit was there; it was felt each time I walked near the garden and the fountain. I could see and hear her laughing and talking and later looking longingly down the Lake as she had done so often in those last days, but I could sense and feel the happiness she now knew that she was resting in one of the most beautiful spots in Michigan - she was home.

Originally, this area at the Point was her husband's family's summer home, one of the places where as children we saw gracing the beach while we walked along. As young and curious girls we had wondered about it so often, that little place on the corner of Graham's Point - the one with the vast view of the landscape. "What went on in that summer house and who were those people who came during the summer months?" we asked ourselves in those summer days.

This is the same home, "The Cottage," where she passed away in the dining room overlooking the same view down Lake Michigan. The Garden now has that view and she now shares that breathtaking view that spans the Great Lakes and is found nowhere else in the world. This truly is God's country, and the place that would be happiness for her and is her gift of happiness for us - the place we know will always be available to us.

"The Cottage" had been her temporary home of sorts during her battle with Cancer. The Garden would be her place of rest, plans she had made herself and was happy with considering the situation. This was a quality of hers, to be "satisfied and happy with the way things were," coming to grips with the reality of her situation long before any of the rest of us could fathom this was really happening to the "youngest" in the family.

It is an illusion to think that more comfort means more happiness. Happiness comes from the capacity to feel deeply, to enjoy simply, to think freely, to be needed.

Storm Jamison

She had now passed three years before this reunion, but in many ways no passing had taken place only a new position had been made for her. Her place at the Point will remain even after the sign of her namesake is removed from the house. She has left too many gifts to leave us at all.

The sunrises coming up off The Island are breathtaking and bring happiness to her garden. The sunsets down Lake Michigan to the West are more of the same. The vastness-of-the-Lakes almost make the horizon and the sunsets seem mystical and closer than they really are to the naked eye. This is her happiness because this is what made her peaceful, and this is how she showed us the true value of happiness as she prepared to pass to her new place. The beauty of God's world and all it inhabits were left for us too.

I had some closure at that time because she was sleeping slightly in my dreams and her spirit was alive and well there too, and surely not at rest. You could feel her presence there, just as I had felt her in my room that day, soon after her burial. We all knew she was happy for our being together at this time when we could find delight in the graduation events and memories of her in more contented times. We now knew what "she is in peace now" meant, and that grief was for those left behind. We now knew that the ache in the heart would remain for a very long time, and many times it would be stirred up even more, but that is life, and that is what living is about and none of us want to miss it. It is a happy time in a sense because we become alive again because of the tragedy.

Also, we could now talk about her freely and happily. That was one of her precious gifts, to be happy with you. It was no longer awkward to mention her name or find joy or happiness in life or feel guilty that she was missing something. She was alive in us. The celebration of her life and all its accomplishments was now. We all knew she was there because her spirit made itself known to us and the sun shone brightly the day of the big party on the Lake, even when the forecast was "a chance for showers." There was a lot of laughter and many friends and family attended. She had taken care of her part in planning this party; she brought the sunshine and warmth to a week that had been cooler, and with rain. It was a party of celebration for her first son's graduation, a celebration for all of us of coming out of grief and of living faith that it was now the right thing to do – be happy.

Happiness is reflective, like the light of heaven.

Washington Irving

Many of the people that attended were friends of our parents, many I had not seen in years, maybe even since high school some 30 years earlier. Her husband's family, her high school friends who have now become my friends too also attended and of course her boys' friends, our relatives and a few extras made up the approximately 200 people who came to the Point that day to celebrate life. All of them have known heartache; living in small town Americana is no protection against loss and sadness. All of them had known sadness, but all of them were ready for the gift of happiness they knew they would find at her "Place at the Point."

So many fond memories flooded back to me as those people appeared. There was the old Judge and his wife who had been her former neighbors, and friends from the "block party planning" days - a time of true happiness for her as the chair of the planning committee. There was the "old salt" whose large sailboat gave us as a family a beautiful July 4th night on the Bay many years earlier to watch fireworks from at least three locations – a time of peace and happiness too. There were her classmates who always had a story about her and who had brought her much happiness; they continue to give that happiness to her family left behind.

The graduation celebration party was just the way she would have wanted it, a few extras at any party in the Upper Peninsula of Michigan is expected. The more the merrier, everyone is welcome – invitations not required. She would have liked it no other way, including welcoming those who just came for free food and beer.

I could let her physical self go that week since I knew her spirit would always be with me and continue to bring me great happiness. She had left a presence, a legacy that was wit, charm, love and kindness inside that package of happiness – that special gift. What a wonderful memory so many of us have of her. Her spirit had enhanced many an occasion bringing joy and happiness, and it did this day too.

She gave me the gift of happiness.

*Happiness is nothing more than
good health and a bad memory.*

Dr. Albert Schweitzer

Take time to reflect on your own happiness and the happiness of others who impact your life.

Happiness is a butterfly, which when pursued is always just beyond your grasp, but which, if you will sit down quietly, will light upon you.

Nathanial Hawthorne

CHAPTER FOURTEEN
My Gift to Her:
Taking her Home to Ireland

Where we love is home – home that our
feet may leave, but not our hearts.

Oliver Wendell Holmes

My sister had always wanted to go to Grand Old Ireland, to the "heart" and homeland of the Irish, the "roots" of our Irish heritage, the Emerald Isle. She had always wanted to see the place where our great-great grandfather had immigrated from in the mid 1800's, going then to Canada before coming in to the USA via Michigan. She had always wanted to be able to tell stories of the place where St. Cronan was seen on many a building, and Cronan, our namesake, was as common as the grand steeples of magnificent churches, or as common as Guinness beer and raucous laughter anytime of the day or night.

I knew I had to take her spirit and essence with me when the blessing of such a wonderful vacation came to be for me four years after her passing. That spring when I was able to take a 12 day vacation to Ireland with my special friend, and live the adventure for my sister too was a tremendously emotional time – almost a surreal time as I packed in silence trying to anticipate the events that lay ahead. This was as much a coming home to Ireland for her and the rest of my immediate family as it was for me. I was going to be the first of our immediate family to touch the Isle's mysterious and rugged shoreline; I knew I had to live each moment to the fullest.

Patricia L. Brooks

We planned an extensive itinerary by researching many books, working closely for months with a travel agent and searching long hours on the Internet while talking to everyone we could that had been there before us. We wanted to visualize a successful trip and then live it with every ounce of our being. We made sure we had all the email and postal mail addresses in our possession that we could possibly need as we headed out on this wondrous adventure, our first trip across the Atlantic.

My luggage also included two cameras, lots of film and two journals. One for writing my thoughts and feelings every night as a reflective journal and documentation, and one for recording purchases and expenses since we were on a bit of a budget. I did not want to miss anything on this trip, and to always be able to cherish it for her and for me.

Even on the flight over on Air Lingus, the Irish Airlines, I knew she was coming along. Everything fell into place for us to go on this trip, even though the United States had entered into war in Iraq only weeks earlier and another terrorism attack was possible, we forged ahead. The country was on high alert, but God held our hands and we made the journey successfully and with great anticipation. I could not sleep on the plane, and thought many times of her presence, especially as we finished our last leg over the Atlantic and saw the spectacular sunrise as we continued east to the Island of Green. She had no doubt been with us all the way, she cherished sunrises and sunsets. She was going to be with us on this entire trip – it was in the plan before we ever boarded. That was just like her, never to miss a good time and to make it special!

She was there in spirit as we traversed the country in our little car, driving on the left side of the road, experiencing all that Ireland has to offer, especially the people and the history. I knew I had to leave something of hers there when I visited the place where it all began for us, our great-great grandfather's birthplace, Roscrea, County Tipperary, Ireland. The town was so much of what I had pictured in my mind so many times. It was just the way she would have wanted it to be – green, friendly, sometimes wet, sometimes sunny and breezy, and always welcoming – not a tourist attraction, but a hard-working, friendly town with a rich heritage walk that made me proud to say my maiden name is Cronan, spelled just like it is on that church, and that school and that monastery..

Roscrea is in the center of the country and "off the path" of the trip we had originally planned, yet it was the heart of the trip in so many ways. Roscrea is located about one hour from Dublin to the West and one hour from Shannon to the East, almost as if it has a special place at the heart of the country, yet it is not known to many tourists. Roscrea is one of the oldest cities in Ireland with a lot of history that pertains to our family heritage.

Where is home? Home is where the heart can laugh
without shyness. Home is where the heart's
tears can dry at their own pace.

Vernon G. Baker

It was so perfect when we arrived at this historical site. The few days it really rained, or as the Irish say – "showering and a bit iffy" - were the days we were in Roscrea to find St. Cronan's churches. The churches, both a Catholic Church and an Anglican Church, were close to the St. Cronan's Catholic School and St. Cronan's Monastery with Cronan spelled exactly the way we had always spelled it. I knew I was home to bury her things. I had brought along items that defined her and items she would have chosen.

The items I chose to bury were gifts from her to me, to one of my other sisters and to her husband. They were: a small sterling silver ring with a faded jade green stone, a ring she wore many times and one I can still remember seeing on her pale thin hand in those last days of her physical being; a black and gold pin she loved to wear on her vintage blazers of a miniature sewing machine and sewing accessories, representing the business she had in her home and a business that did very well; a laminated copy of her obituary adorned with her smiling face, which was lovingly written by one of her dear friends; a small refrigerator magnet with a warm saying and a cuddly animal on it, two things she loved, enjoyed and shared; another refrigerator magnet with a poem about living life to the fullest, the philosophy that so described her and was her to the end had to be included; and, last but not least, a copy of her business card with her name, logo and phone number on it, just in case someone digs up these items that were lovingly placed in a Ziploc plastic bag for posterity.

Before venturing to St. Cronan's Catholic Church and cemetery that day, we stopped at the local hardware store and bought the trowel and bag of seeds to plant flowers at her "spot." I enjoyed telling the shopkeeper that my maiden name was Cronan, just like the name on the two churches, school and monastery there in Roscrea, and that we had come "home" to my roots, to bury my sister's things and bring her spirit and essence home. The shopkeeper generously smiled as I talked, and listened intently to everything I said. The Irish are so cordial to the Americans. I went on to tell him we would also investigate baptismal records on my family history. The shopkeeper gave us another warm smile and said "Welcome home and good luck, may God bless." I knew he felt my sense of pride and excitement about this leg of the trip, and that he had heard similar stories before, and that he was always willing to let the Irish from the mainland have their time too. The most beautiful part of Ireland that I will always cherish is the people.

We found the perfect spot for these precious gifts. She would have loved this spot because it was situated high above the church grounds overlooking the little town of Roscrea. It stood out amongst the many Celtic crosses that adorned the gravesites, calling for her to join those already at rest in that plot – the Murphy, Asbury, Cronan clan. It was a spot in the corner of a plot that proudly displayed the Cronan name. There were many plots with the Cronan name on them in this cemetery, but this spot felt like the one where I could say good-bye to her again.

The front door of the old church faced her special place up on the hill with the small river flowing through the lower level of the grounds. We placed her items in the corner of the plot and covered the area with flower seeds, gently making a mark there where life would be visible in a few short weeks when the flowers would sprout from the soil. Spring was coming to Ireland, and a new beginning for this spot was about to take place.

My friend walked ahead of me down the dark concrete stairs of the cemetery and left me there to say good-bye to her on that hill atop Roscrea. "It was a bit iffy," as the Irish like to say, when it is gray skies, drizzling and showering. I could feel a slight chill for the first time that day. Was it a chill from the rain or a chill that I may never pass this way again? I held my hand on the spot on that plot where we left her things, thinking again about putting those items in that plastic bag in the ground, covering the bag with the dirt and seeing her face on the obituary go away in to the earth. My heart was happy with a good feeling that I had done something I had dreamed about for so long, but heavy because of the sadness of her coming to Ireland in this way. I knelt there a long time, saying I love you and good-bye again and again, until my knees ached and I knew I had to stand and leave. I took one more look around the span of the town's view, the church and river below, and the many Celtic crosses, threw her a kiss and hurried to the church's gate unable to look back one more time.

The next member of the family to visit this place will be able to find her as we documented the site in my journal and took many pictures. I was not the first in our extended Cronan family to visit this place, and I am sure with the large Cronan family that we have, will not be the last. She will be looking for all of us to come by her garden spot at the Point in St. Ignace, Michigan, and her spot in Roscrea, County Tipperary, Ireland, as well. Her spirit is in our hearts and in our lives daily as we live in those gifts she gave to us.

We left St. Cronan's Church grounds feeling like we had consummated our journey and that we had done what we needed to do for some closure for me - some sense of moving to the next level of where my sister will always be in my life. The place was so right for her, the setting so perfect and yet so "not-so-perfect" as to remain somewhat untouched. My feeling of starting to let her go came over me as we drove away from those old stone buildings back toward the countryside where we were staying at a wonderful Bed and Breakfast (B and B), just the place she would have chosen had she had the chance to physically travel with us on this journey. Even the (B and B) owner was her style, as was the priest with the quick wit and pink cheeks – it was a grand day for the Irish.

Gifts come in all shapes and sizes, but the gifts of sisterhood have no limits. They are there when you need them, with no price tag and no return policy. They are to be shared, cherished and valued, but most of all, used daily. They are there for the taking and whenever you need them or to sustain you and keep you; they are there even if "until death do you part" becomes a reality.

Ireland was more than we had expected and yet we had expected so much. It was as green as the color Emerald, as misty as the fine shower of spring and as sunny as the many smiles of the Irish people. She knew we were home too because she made sure the angels were on our side; things went very well and without any hitches, and we had a fabulous trip. We embraced every moment of our 12 days, especially our time in Roscrea, County Tipperary, where I said good-bye to her one more time in a special way.

My gift now to my sister is to continue living my life for both of us and to share her gifts in my own life. To remember to practice my faith, to be loving and compassionate, to be grateful for my life just the way it is and to have the courage to live life to the fullest. To accept the gifts God has given me, be patient and tolerant, to appreciate all my friendships and my family and to leave more in this world than I take with me. She taught me to be free for all seasons.

These are the gifts I give to you.

For everything there is a season,
a time to every purpose under Heaven.

The Book of Ecclesiastes

Your ticket out of this journey on to your own is to document for yourself what you learned, what you enjoyed and what you would suggest for yourself as you travel your journey home. God bless!

Home is a place you grow up wanting to leave,
and grow old wanting to get back to.

John E. Pearce

ABOUT THE AUTHOR

An inspirational speaker, Patricia L. Brooks has contributed to the development of successful women for many years. Patricia L. Brooks Seminars, www.plbrooks.com, features topics in Human Relations and Marketing by offering Patricia's business expertise for keynotes and workshops. Her mission is to enhance the spirit of the client's organization.

She has been a university faculty associate for over ten years and is currently teaching Marketing at Arizona State University-East. Patricia has a Masters Degree in Organizational Management, the Advanced Toastmasters designation and was recently named to Who's Who Amongst America's Teachers.

Although Patricia has resided in Arizona for almost 30 years, her heart remains in the Upper Peninsula of Michigan – the setting for "Gifts of Sisterhood" – www.giftsofsisterhood.com. She has operated her business since 1996 and is active in the Arizona Small Business Association.

Patricia began writing her first "memoir" by keeping a diary as a young girl and continued throughout her life to keep reflective journals. She has published articles, written short stories, edited university curriculum and developed a career of seminar presentations. She is a member of the National Association of Women Writers (NAWW), the Phoenix Writers Club (PWC) and Women Writers of the Desert (WWD). She currently makes her home in Scottsdale, Arizona.

Please contact Patricia for speaking engagements at:

Patricia L. Brooks Seminars
7970 E. Camelback Rd.
Suite 710
Scottsdale, AZ 85251
480-250-5556 cell phone
patricia@plbrooks.com
www.plbrooks.com

For more books use:
www.giftsofsisterhood.com
and
www.authorhouse.com

Printed in the United States
145146LV00001B/13/A